# CONCRETE MARSHMALLOWS AND THE HOME SWEET HOME CAFÉ

A Business Fable

Copyright © 2019, Edward J. McShane

For Lisa Coast

**CHAPTER ONE**

My name is Fred.

I'm about to tell you the story of how my life changed forever.

I've spent most of my career in sales and customer service. There were endless months of windshield miles. By the time I was 36, I had been on the road for seventeen years. I saw the inside of more hotel rooms, conference rooms, restaurants, and rental cars than I can count. And I was good at what I did—really good. I received regional, state, and national sales and customer service awards, customers liked me, and I brought in a great deal of business.

But that life can be tough. After one divorce and a few years to think about it, I was ready to get off the road. My life had begun to change. I had the feeling I was losing a step or two.

Contemplating a search for a new position in another company, the general manager asked me to come into her office. She told me a district management position had opened in sales and customer services and asked if I was interested in the job. I told her that, yes, I absolutely was. She knew I wanted to be a supervisor. I figured I could look at spreadsheets, pie charts, and time cards as well as anybody else. I was confident I could hustle people in and out of the door while making sure they did their jobs. Two conversations and an interview later, she hired me as a Regional Manager.

I was in.

The job wasn't hard. I'd walk around, run into my staff and say, "Hey, how'd that sale go? Everything okay with you?" I'd talk it up. I made it a point to ask everybody how they were doing and if there was anything they needed from me. But it was just background noise. It was as if I was looking at a baseball game from the third row behind the on-deck circle, waiting for a guy to come up so I could chant, "Hey batter, batter, hey batter, batter... swing!" I thought chatter would help him get a hit. I was attempting to connect with my staff, but it was just something for me to do, to make me feel like I was contributing, and to let them know I was around.

I'd attend weekly meetings with the higher-ups where they would tell me what I needed to do to "make those sales happen." Then I'd tune out as they droned on about the corporate atmosphere, the mission of the company, their golf score, or whatever. About once a quarter, it was my turn to do the droning. I had to get up in front of all these managers and executives and tell them my perspective on "the workforce as a team" and how we could all "become a family within the firm," making sure I was hitting all the right notes in my talk.

It was death. I was going through the motions, delivering the same speech every three months. It was always "How to Connect with Your Customer and Your Staff." I'd discuss repeatedly the importance of relationships, or "caring," when it came to sales, customer service, and relationships with your staff and peers. I believed what I was saying, but after a while I was just mouthing the words. I stayed current by going over whatever was popular in current literature on the subject. Much of my quarterly boardroom chats was entirely forgettable, but it had to be done.

Although the speeches I gave felt pointless, I truly knew the meat behind sales and customer service. Relationships make your success, not whatever new trend is being pushed by the next trainer, motivational speaker, or business journal. I didn't win all those sales and customer service awards for nothing. When people feel that you know, understand and genuinely like them, they are far more inclined to listen to what you have to say, and to buy what you are selling. Being a manager appeared to involve the same skills—having a relationship with your staff made things easier. Guided by a supportive and responsive manager, the sales staff felt better about their jobs. My sales and customer service staff were great; they made my job a piece of cake. Though sales had been off for several quarters, management explained that this was due to a change in the marketplace. OK, I thought, at least it is not me.

I became a "hands-off" manager. I never wanted my staff to be called into my office for anything. I wanted them to go about their business, independent of my interference. And, like I said, I was lucky. My staff managed themselves. Whenever somebody new came to the office, I let them know straight out of the box what kind of numbers they had to produce. That was about all anybody needed to know. Everybody ran with that directive and they all came through.

But I didn't know my staff very well. I was acquainted with them, but our relationship was distant, "professional" I suppose, but I wasn't in tune with the nuances that each person presented. I let their numbers be my guide with no grasp on who they were. I became distant to how they operated and approached their customer, management, and their peers, all of whom were windows into who they were. Giving them space kept me on the perimeter of their jobs, which eventually led to a distinct drawback in my ability to reach them. They came to me less and less for help, and our relationships became distant.

When I first started out twenty something years ago, I had a knack for what to say, how and when to say it, and when to keep my mouth shut. I cared more about people, and that superseded the sale. I was good at it. But lately, I wasn't sure what "it" was anymore. It seemed like so many changes were taking place in my life. Time had been marching on, and with it came a technology shift. Having been off the front lines of sales for so long, I got stale. When my staff came to me for help, my old battle stories from the road began to sound stale, even to my ears. They lacked punch. Given the reaction from my staff, they didn't seem to have any relevance to them. I could see in their eyes that I wasn't connecting. Their expressions were flat. And I'd always hear, "OK, well, thanks a lot," which was equivalent to "I'm not even sure why I asked you the question in the first place." Sales were slow, but I was again told it was due to changes in the marketplace.

To be honest, I don't think any of this mattered to me; I was on cruise control. My job was set and life was good, despite this vague feeling of distance between myself, my other managers, my staff, and the customers. But the staff seemed happy. My bosses had left me alone. It had been almost four years since my move to management as a supervisor. There was no looking back.

## CHAPTER TWO

The first thing Monday morning, I got a call from my boss, the Regional Manager. I would usually see this guy once a week, if that often. As long as everything was going well on my end, he never bothered me. I liked it that way. I never needed his attention. In general, an employee never initiates a meeting with their boss. Nobody ever calls and says, "Hey, I don't think you and I have had enough meetings this week. How about I come into your office so you can talk to me about things?" That never happens. It's always the other way around. They always call you.

He said, "Hey, Fred, can you come into my office for a few minutes? I have something I want to talk to you about." He'd been my Regional Manager for about two, maybe three years, and we got along fine.

But, when I got a call saying he wanted to speak to me for no apparent reason that I was aware of, I had an awful feeling.

I went in and sat down in the chair in front of his desk. "Hey, Fred, good to see you." His expression was flat. He was smiling, but there was nothing behind his eyes. I nodded my head without moving in the seat.

"Fred, we've decided to make a few changes and I wanted to tell you first. The good news is you're not losing your job."

Then he brought the hammer down: "The bad news is that you're being demoted."

I looked at the floor. Then looked back at him.

"Fred, we need to eliminate a couple of District Managers. Those jobs will fall to me. You're going to have to join your team and get back on the street. The sales have been stagnant, and we need to bring those back up. With your experience, you're the best one we could think of to get things moving for the company again. But, hey, that should be a piece of cake for you, right?"

"Umm…yeah, I guess so," I said, wondering if this was going to be permanent.

"Don't worry about the salary part. You'll keep your base for thirty days, but then you'll be working against the draw. But, again, with your background, you'll do fine. Remember what we used to say: 'Sales is where the money is.' Right, Fred?"

"Yeah…right." I resisted the urge to grab my chest. I felt short of breath and an ache ran across my ribs. It wasn't a familiar pain. Nothing I'd ever experienced physically had felt like this. Maybe this was an anxiety attack; I wasn't sure. I caught only the last few words of his sentence. He said, "So, I'll have Human Resources set you up with the new paperwork. They'll send that over to you today. You'll do great, Fred; I just know it." He smiled this big cheesy smile and stuck out his hand. I shook it, but my hand felt limp, so I squeezed a little harder.

My feet took me to my desk, but I didn't feel them hit the floor. My staff glanced at me and then went back to their phones. I dropped into my chair like I had been shot. All kind of thoughts ran through my head, the most prominent being, "Is this guy trying to get rid of me?" I wasn't sure what to think. Sales are "stagnant" so he puts me back on the street to turn things around. Huh? Something about this doesn't make sense.

Damn. I had to get back out and sell. Meet the customers again. It had been so long. I stared at the wall for what seemed like hours. This was all so familiar. I've seen the worst case scenario happen before. A manager gets demoted and they eventually kick him out the door.

I needed to make sure this didn't happen. I was OK financially, but I needed to keep my job. I wanted to go back to management. I didn't want to go backwards. And now, for the first time in years, I wasn't sure if I still knew how to speak to people let alone how to make a sale.

## CHAPTER THREE

I was immobilized. I tried to take a deep breath, but the air wouldn't come all the way into my lungs. Staring at the blank screen of my computer, all I could see was my reflection. I looked gray, completely spent.

I had no idea what to do. I assumed I'd receive some leads from my boss at some point, but that was the least of my worries. A fog of self-doubt had rolled in my office, and the walls seemed to be inching toward me.

I grabbed for my phone. I had to talk to somebody, and right now. I needed to clear my head and take the energy out of this mood. I made a couple of calls and left a few voicemail messages of the, "Hey, how are you doing, just thinking about you, let's go get a cup of coffee," variety. But I didn't really want to get a cup of coffee with anybody. I just wanted this feeling to go away. I wanted to feel like I was somebody again.

I looked down at my phone and started typing in a friend's name. But instead of his name, another name came up. It was the therapist my ex-wife and I spoke to when we were going through our divorce. I hadn't seen him in years.

I really liked this guy. Apart from being a therapist, he has done a great deal business coaching and consulting. He knew his way around the dynamics of the industry. He was funny and kind. He said he wanted the people who came to his office to have "a soft place to land." He was a smart, but normal guy.

I called him. He gave me an appointment for that night.

He opened the door and shook my hand like I was his best friend and he hadn't seen me since high school. He was always like that, and even though it seemed a little strong this time, maybe due to my vulnerable state, I really appreciated him being so warm.

I told him what happened earlier in the day, about getting called into the boss's office, about how it made my stomach feel and about how I felt lost. I didn't know what to do. I was hoping he could help me sort through this emotional mess, from both a business and personal perspective. I needed to get back to my old self and hit the ground running tomorrow.

In response, he asked a question I wished he had kept to himself. "Fred, can you remember ever having felt like this before?" Nothing came to mind immediately, but then my thoughts drifted back to the time I had seen him last. My stomach, which had just begun to settle down, regained that awful sick feeling. I dropped my chin and, looking at the floor of his office, said two words: "My divorce."

"Fred," he said, "I'm not asking you to dredge up any of the old pain, but what you're going through now is a lot like what you went through a few years ago. Fred, this is a big disconnection. At the very least, it's a significant change."

I kept staring at the ground. He was absolutely right. My professional identity had been amputated and I had suddenly been jettisoned backwards into a role I no longer knew. I needed him to tell me what my next move was supposed to be. This man knew more about me than I had recalled. He must have recognized that look in my eyes because, before I could speak, he said, "Fred, do you remember what I asked you to do the last time you were in my office? You know, after the divorce?"

I didn't. I looked up at him and shook my head from side to side, with what must have been a pleading expression on my face. Before I could say anything, he said, "I asked you to make attempts to get outside of yourself." I began to remember what he'd said years ago. At that time he implied I was self-centered. I was more concerned about the superficial impressions I could make to others than being invested in the love I showed to my wife.

I told him I remembered the stuff about being self centered but not about him telling me to "get outside of myself." He smiled and said, "That's entirely understandable. When people are going through a loss or very significant change in their lives, sometimes information is difficult to remember. What I suggested was that you find a cause, or somebody that you could use your service."

I remembered the advice. I rejected it then. And I wasn't happy that he brought it up again.

In fact, this annoyed me.

I said, "I don't mean to sound like a jerk, but I came here to get some help in ridding myself of this pain and moving forth in a new direction. I need some clarity. So I'm a little confused as to how my doing something for somebody else is going to help me do a better job. I'm just not getting this." He could tell I was being a little terse, and even rude.

The therapist looked back into my eyes and smiled a little. "I totally understand, Fred, but let me clarify. Giving of yourself when you're feeling this lousy provides you two important things that you need right now to get outside of yourself. The first is perspective. The other is meaning."

Something about his tone made me lean in. He went on. "In order to do that, it's important that you focus on what you can do for another person. You have to practice changing your perspective." He paused. "Pain tends to draw you in."

"When you're depressed, anxious, disappointed, or hurt in any way, it's very easy and almost natural to focus on what hurts, dwelling on how badly you feel. As a result, you do what you can to address whatever hurts."

"Because," he continued, "you have just received such a blow, getting your life back is your first priority. But to do that, you must adjust your focus away from your pain and look at how you can ease the pain of another. Giving helps you feel better because, if nothing else, you're connecting with another person. To begin with, try two things: first, practice what you can do for the people around you. Start with your friends, your family, and especially your coworkers. Be of service to them. You will begin to see the fog lift and your feelings normalize. You will feel a renewed sense of meaning and purpose."

"It will not only help you become a better salesman, it will-and forgive me for being so blunt-be a better, more grounded, and happier person altogether."

I paused for a long time, unsure if he was expecting me to say something. The silence was thick. I hoped he would say something else that added a little more ballast to this concept. When it became clear he was finished, I felt the disappointment threatening to choke me. I needed him to tell me what to do for *me* and *my* problems. And the solution was to help somebody else? That was pure nonsense.

"So, you're telling me that, in order to sell better, develop a client base, and respond to people better, I have to be nice to my people, beginning with those in my inner circle? I think I do this already. I'm not an insufferable jerk. You now want me to send them all 'love notes?'"

"Well, that might be part of it." He smiled at my snide tone. Nothing I said seemed to faze him. Told you he was a good guy.

After another longer pause, I said, "So, can you tell me the other part of it?"

"Sure." He pointed to a hand-painted sign hanging over the door. I turned my head to study the words: "Come with me to a quiet place and rest." Unimpressed, I asked, "Did you make that up?"

"No, that's been around a long time." he said, chuckling and shaking his head. "This is what I try to do when people are with me. I try to help them find peace. In order for them to feel safe, to feel that they'll be OK, they have to feel peace. Ultimately, although I do what I can to help facilitate the process, that quiet has to come from within each individual person."

"They have to make it a centerpiece of their day and, by helping others find their peace, you begin to find it within yourself. I'm sure you have it within you, too. I want you to find that peace again."

"My hope is for you to be able to reconnect from that place of peace with all the people in your life-your customers, your colleagues, your friends and family-in a deeper, more meaningful way. If you do this, I guarantee you your success in business and your personal life will improve in ways that are hard to imagine."

I nodded. I appreciated all that he had to tell me, I really did. But inwardly, I cringed. This still wouldn't help me make a sale like, oh, in the next twenty-four hours. Tomorrow morning I would be joining a group of people I had just finished supervising, and I'd be slugging it out with every one of them over the same sale. A chill of anxiety traveled up my spine, and I blurted out, "Look, I appreciate this, but I have a great deal of trepidation going to work in the morning, and…." I stopped and felt the words catch in my throat. "I don't know if I can do this. It's been awhile. It's sales and communication that I'm not that sure about. And then there's customer service, let alone interpersonal relationships, that I'm even less sure about." I let out a deep breath and stared at the floor. "I'm not sure I know how to talk to people anymore, let alone connect with them on the level you're asking me to do."

Taking a deep breath, I said, "Don't get me wrong," I hurried on, looking back at him. "This is all fantastic, but I need something a little more concrete than this idea to get me through the next few months." I'm not sure what compelled me to continue, but I blurted out, "It's as if I need to be shown how to do all of this stuff all over again."

My therapist leaned forward in his chair and nodded enthusiastically, looking almost as if he had known what I was going to say. "I know. You do."

"I do *what*? I said.

"You need to be shown how to "do this stuff," as you say, all over again. You need to start over. You need a new beginning."

"You have to begin to believe in yourself, but first you have to get outside of yourself and focus on those around you. Care about others, Fred. That's what sales, customer service and the essence of what a human relationship is all about. First, start with your staff."

He adjusted himself in his chair and said, "Go into the office tomorrow and tell them, "Well, folks, I guess I'm one of you now. I just want to thank you for being such a great sales and customer service staff…and I hope I can be as good as all of you have been." It lets them know you are human. They will see your heart. And they will respond with warmth." I pondered his suggestion. Saying that to my staff would make me feel like such a failure. But I made a mental note to say it anyway.

"Thanks," I said. It was all I could think of saying. I looked at the floor and stayed quiet. After a moment, I stammered. "I truly do feel like I'm at the beginning again. I think I've lost a step, you know?"

Then he said something that would change my life.

"I think you need a little help to go further, to get that extra step. I'm asking you to change your focus and your philosophy, and that's hard to do on your own."

"What you may need, at least as I see it, is a mentor. I know somebody, if you're interested. She can help. She's an expert in the field. She has mentored others who have been in the same place you are right now. She coaches those that don't know what to say to people, that don't feel confident in what to say, and have waning confidence in their sales and customer service abilities." He stopped for a second, got up and went to his desk. He opened a drawer, pulled out a business card, and held it in his hand. "And she is the embodiment of the philosophy I've just introduced to you. Watch how she engages people. She could change your life."

"Oh, great," I said sarcastically, wondering whom he had in mind. *A sales coach? Another therapist?* Feeling down, I wasn't ready to confide in somebody else. Then he continued.

"I know it's a big step, but she's the best at what she does," he reassured me. "People from all over stop in and visit with her. She connects with people like no other. She has an amazing ability to engage, and makes people feel valued, understood, listened to, and loved."

"And her formula for communication will change your business and interpersonal relationships permanently. She's shown it to me, and I've seen her in action. It's exactly what you need."

"OK," I said, thinking this woman might have something to show me. Still, I'm not quite ready. But I figure I'll check her out, at least once, and see what she can offer. I stood there I wondering how much it costs to hire her as a consultant. "Sorry for asking, but does she charge for her services?" When they are this good, these kinds of consultants don't come cheap.

"Yes, and no," he explained. "Your fee will be to carry forward the message she offers you. And while you're with her, you might try the Chicken Fried Steak."

"Excuse me?" I had no idea what he was talking about.

"She runs a restaurant. A breakfast and lunch place."

Then his words hit me. "Wait," I said. "This woman runs a restaurant?" He had to be kidding. Seriously?

"Yep. The Home Sweet Home Café-the best in town. And her name is not 'this woman.' It's Lisa. I'll call her. She's been a friend of mine for years, and I'm sure she'll help you. But promise me: Do what she says and pay close attention to not just what she does, but how she does it. People really like her food, but they *love* Lisa. They keep coming back because of the person she is. She makes people feel special, like they are one of her family. She's the best at customer service of anyone I've ever seen. And she's one of the best human beings I've ever known. She can teach you everything you need to know to get back on your feet in your career, Fred."

He handed me her card. I promised him I would call her tomorrow.

"Don't worry, Fred. Just show up for lunch. You'll recognize her by the smile on her face and that she's always in motion. I'll let her know you'll be there. And, with your permission, I'll let her know we spoke and the nature of your difficulties. She'll want to know, and I'll tell her what you and I have discussed, if that's OK with you."

I told him that was fine, signed some kind of disclosure form, shook his hand, and left his office. I switched myself on auto-pilot, drove home, and sat in my car in the driveway processing the past hour. I still had to go to work tomorrow and face my coworkers, and he recommended that in order to turn around my professional career, I call some lady that makes a mean Chicken Fried Steak and sit and watch her pour coffee?

I hope she's everything he says she is.

Otherwise, I'm completely screwed.

## CHAPTER FOUR

I got out of bed, took a shower, went to the mirror and stood there. I looked like death. I averted my eyes and got dressed. I didn't want to remember this expression.

By the time I got to my office, my staff had already arrived. I asked for their attention, gave them the news, smiled weakly, and thanked them for being so good at what they did. I offered my help, and I asked for theirs. The responses surprised me. They were unreasonably considerate with their support. A couple of them came up to me, patted me on the shoulder and reached in for a hug. When I saw more of them drawing closer, I turned and went directly to my desk. A few more seconds and I would have lost it. Crying has never been my thing, and I wasn't going to shed any tears today. My new professional life was starting and I am supposed to meet this "Lisa" person to show me how to be amazing.

Whatever.

I left the office around noon and showed up at the Home Sweet Home Café. A few tables and some stools at the counter were open. I sat at the counter and looked for somebody fitting Lisa's description: Always in motion, a smile on her face.

I saw her immediately. At least that's what I thought I saw. She was there and, in a second, gone to another customer. Then, with a deliberate pause and a graceful posture, she stood and spoke to the folks at the table just behind me. Never hurried, never distracted. She seemed to take pleasure in taking her time. With a light, fast step, she was gone behind the counter to pick up an order from the cooks.

As I watched her with interest, her eyes caught mine and she said, "Hold on one second, I'll be right there."

Just then I noticed that she was the only waitress working in the restaurant. She was manning all the tables and stools at the counter by herself.

"OK, sorry for the wait. What can I get you?" A huge smile. A genuine smile, too. She projected sincerity. And she looked right at me. It took me by surprise. Her energy was palpable.

The woman definitely had a presence about her. Given her pace, as she flew around the restaurant, I thought she'd at least be a little winded. Instead, when we met, she was poised, smiling, and looked straight into my eyes.

"My name's Fred. I was told you were expecting me."

"Oh, of course. Fred, it's nice to meet you. I'm Lisa. Tell you what, I have two girls coming in shortly. As soon as they get here, how about we take a few minutes in one of the open booths to talk? Would you like a cup of coffee?"

I nodded, then she handed me a cup and directed me to a booth in the back. I settled in and waited for her staff to show up. When they got there, she joined me.

"Fred," she said as I added the first of three creamers into my cup, "I tend to jump right in with the folks that I work with. I have a Six-Point Program that I'll be teaching you in the time we're together. So, to begin this process, I want you to just watch and experience this place. "Watch" and "Experience" are the first two points of the program, but they are closely linked. Anyway, I'll explain that later in more detail. For now, just watch and experience everything going on in here. Breathe it in, then tell me what you see." She quickly returned to her customers.

Before I could say, "Nice to meet you," I was alone again and studying her place. There were signs on the wall with quotes everywhere: "Cherish Life's Simple Treasures," "Friends and Family Gather Here," "Someone Else Is Happy with Less Than What You Have," "Stressed spelled backwards is Desserts," and, my favorite, "Maybe It's Not Home Sweet Home. Adjust."

When she came back and sat with me, she asked me what I "watched" and "experienced." In response I said, perhaps a bit too eagerly, "I see a really great place here."

She smiled and said, "Well, that's not exactly what I was looking for, but I'm sure you're trainable." I didn't know what she meant by that, and it ticked me off a little. I wasn't sure I liked her, and here I was supposed to be mentored by this person. She seemed a little patronizing. I thought, "Doesn't she know who I am?"

She said, "Let me back up a bit. I understand that you could use a little regeneration of your spirit." Now I'm feeling a little defensive. On the one hand, I was really impressed that she used the phrase, "regeneration of your spirit," but that was a little too close too quick, and I was immediately uneasy. She may have zeroed in on precisely what I was after, but my guard went up.

I responded, "No, not exactly. I came here because I was told you have some insight into how I could fine tune my sales and customer service and improve my relationships with people in general." My words felt a little hollow, and Lisa took some time to respond. I again wondered why I had consented to come here.

Then Lisa said, "Fred, you're going to get a little of the background and theory of my approach, and then I'm going to tell you about my Six-Point Program. You are about to begin, for lack of a better phrase, a kind of spiritual journey. Practical, to be sure, but I am also going to help you find yourself again. I'm going to help you get back the skills and techniques you may have lost. And when you're done with me, you will have better success in any of the best years of your sales and customer service career. I'm sure of it."

"Most of all," she said, "you will find that you'll begin to care again. The people in front of you will matter."

I was dumbfounded. She had just promised me that I was going to be as successful as I had ever been in my life. And she ran a restaurant with a capacity of maybe sixty people. Although she was very charming and certainly had a distinct presence, I was skeptical that she was up to the task of getting me back to the place I'd been.

She must have seen the bewildered look on my face, because she smiled and said, "Fred, I'm sure you are great at selling, and I'm sure you've had years of success in customer service. I am positive that I can't teach you anything about your career. My job is to take you on a little bit of a walk down your *own* path. I have no doubt about your skills, but it's your confidence I'm a little concerned about. My job, in part, is to help you get your life back. To believe in yourself again."

Still a little miffed, I said somewhat tersely "You're going to help me do all that, huh?" I knew I was being dismissive but, hey, put yourself in my shoes. I thought we were going to talk business over a cup of coffee and now I'm about to attend a seminar on "Getting Your Mojo Back." I've been to dozens of these training seminars—one big blowhard after another gets up on a stage with a bad PowerPoint presentation to try to get me motivated and excited about life. Oh, please. That "be a better person" and "just believe in yourself" stuff lasts about as long as it takes you to leave the meeting and get back to your desk, when reality and the deadlines sets in.

Undeterred, Lisa continued her line of thought. "Well, after a fashion, I am. You will learn to refine your people skills, one person at a time. And you're going to have to give me the time I request during the next few weeks. By the time you're done, you'll be attentive, responsive, and alert to the needs of your customers and your staff. You will listen better than you ever have, leaning in to their needs and respond with nuance and understanding. You'll know exactly what to do." She smiled and said, "But, before we get started, I want you to know what I base my teachings on. See that sign?"

She pointed to a sign on the wall above a row of tables near the door. It said, "Do Unto Others as You Would Have Done unto You." She looked at me and said, "Everything you will learn is based on that. It is the Golden Rule." I nodded my head, and she said, "Fred, what exactly does that mean to you?" I was caught a little off guard, so after stumbling for a word or two, I said something along the lines of, "You should treat people nicely?"

"Well," she said, "it depends on what you define as "nicely." She stopped for a minute, walked over to the sign, pointed up at it, and said, "In every way you treat other people, you reference how you wish to be treated. It is a general rule, I admit, but it is perhaps the most pervasive spiritual tenet known to mankind. It is one we too often forget."

Lisa stood up and started to wipe down a counter. "Usually, we want things our way. We want to see things unfold under our influence and control. When you're in customer service, or when you speak to your colleagues, that doesn't always work. Your responsibility is to find out the needs of another person and, in that regard, how you go about determining what their needs might be. The Golden Rule helps you establish that clearly and with understanding."

I must have looked like a deer in the headlights, because she continued, "I'm not a mind reader. And the Golden Rule doesn't assume that you are, either. It just reminds you to be aware of one simple question: How would you want to be treated in any encounter with another individual?" I stood there with what must have been an unknowing expression on my face.

"The answer is that you wish to be treated with respect but, moreover, with patience and kindness. Patience and Kindness."

I thought about that for a moment. I knew it sounded familiar. I couldn't put my finger on where I'd heard it before, so I asked, "Excuse me, Lisa, but that 'patience and kindness' thing. Is that in the Golden Rule?"

"No." Lisa said, grabbing some silverware and a napkin. "First Corinthians. "Love is Patient, Love is Kind. That's the *foundation* of the Golden Rule. You love these people as you would want to be loved. You remain patient and remain kind. You must always communicate respect. You may not know everything about the person, and you may not be able to respond to every single one of their needs, but if you maintain the Golden Rule, if you do to them as you would have done to you, you will create and keep firmly established your interpersonal foundation. Everything that I will teach you through my Six Point Program comes from that philosophy."

Lisa smiled and said, "It's been nice to meet you, Fred. I would like to see you at eight in the morning, for one hour. Then, after that, we'll meet weekly. But tomorrow, be here at eight, sharp. That's when the six-point program begins."

I shook her hand, got into my car, and drove to the office. Sitting at my desk, I realized that the cynicism I had was gone. Instead, I was just staring at my phone, wondering, "What am I supposed to do now?" I reached for my calendar and put "Lisa, eight a.m." on tomorrow's date. Five minutes went by and I was still looking at the calendar.

Man, I hope she can help me.

## CHAPTER FIVE

The next morning I called my boss and told him that I would be a little late. He seemed OK with it, so I went right to the restaurant. I showed up at 8:00. Lisa was the only one working the place and there were a few people scattered around the restaurant. As soon as I came through the door, she caught my eye and said, "Fred, good morning. Come here for a second," gesturing to where she stood behind the counter. As I sheepishly inched behind the cash register and made my way past the coffee pot and the service trays, I saw her reaching for something. It was a black piece of cloth with a long ribbon on it. She thrust it towards me with her right hand and said, "Here. Put this on." I noticed that she was wearing something just like it.

It was an apron.

The woman had just handed me an apron.

"Seriously?" I asked, holding this thing away from me with my thumb and forefinger as if it was infected.

"Seriously." And she said it with a tone that could only be described as "nice." She was firm, but she was distinctly pleasant. "This is what I'm going to have you do. For the time we are together, you're going to work for me. I'm going to show you the most fundamental aspect of customer service and sales: how to engage people. You'll begin to re-establish yourself as somebody you really want to be. You'll rediscover your voice."

"But, first, let me show you something." She brought out a big photo album—a huge book- and laid it out on the counter. "Fred, I know when you came in here, you saw some woman flying around the restaurant. You came on blind faith that I could help you, and you see this pretty strange environment for training that I'm sure you never expected." I smiled and thought, "Well, duh. Didn't exactly mistake this place for the Wharton School of Business."

She continued and opened the big book. She said, "I thought I'd start out by sharing with you some of my experiences. In this book are pictures and letters from dozens of people whom I have helped, people who were once in the position you're in right now. They said that if anybody has any questions about my process, they are happy to share what help I have given them" As we started paging through the book, I couldn't believe the pictures I was seeing and the people she had helped. If I told you who they were, you would fall off your chair.

I was dumbfounded. The people who had come to Lisa for help were national and international names of renown.

I looked back down at the book, then up at Lisa. It seemed inexplicable that this woman would have coached so many people, so many respected professionals from all different disciplines. So I had to ask. "How did this start? I mean, how did you begin this process? Did you have any background going into this, or was this something you developed over time?" I wanted to be careful not to offend her, but I was dying to know how this all began.

Keeping her hand on the album and her eyes on the pictures, Lisa said, "My father was the Chairman of the Board of a Fortune 500 company. In the late seventies and early eighties, under his leadership, each quarter was more profitable than the last. I was told that an MBA student did his thesis on my father's work."

"Well," she said, "I'm his youngest daughter. Some of what I learned was by observation, listening to him on the phone, talking to him the few times he was home. Some was from my own education in business, finance, that kind of thing."

"My father, although a tough task master, was a kind and considerate man. He told me that, throughout his entire career in business, the thing he was most proud of was getting pensions for his clerical and administrative staff. He said he had to petition his Board for a year to get that, but he would say that "those people carried the business on their shoulders."

"I always remembered that. He treated people like he wanted to be treated."

"And my father came up through sales. He was hired as the National Sales Manager of his firm when I was three years old. He was an amazing salesman. He never completed college. He took graduate courses in Accounting, Business and Finance at Northwestern. He absorbed and applied the coursework and he was a great manager, but he knew that personal relationships in sales and customer service, was, as he'd say, "the engine that drives the train."

"And he knew that sales were solely based on the relationship you have with the customer and your colleagues. Everything was relational. It wasn't manipulation. He never wanted to coerce people in any way. He wanted his sales force to be genuinely good people, and hired those that fit his mold of being kind, considerate and respectful. Smart and informed, but also a person that embodied a spirit of friendship and, frankly, love. They were representative of a company that could facilitate and further a good living for distributors and customers. He felt business was the platform to improve people's lives, and a relationship of care and honest consideration was fundamental to that end."

"So," she said, closing the pages and placing her hand on the cover of the book, "I developed my own style of management, based on my education, experience, and conversations with my father. After I bought the restaurant, one of my father's colleagues referred me my first client. His colleague had known me through the years and was impressed how I helped a young man struggling in his relationship skills. I just showed him what I knew, and I knew this." She stretched her arm outward and scanned it across the restaurant. "Three months later, this man got a promotion. Shortly thereafter, my father's colleague referred a two more folks, then the word got out."

Pointing back at the album of photos, I said, "These people worked here, and you helped all of them?" Humbly, she said, "Well, yes, I did. I just walked them through the six steps, and they found their voice just like you're going to find yours."

My entire thinking changed. Lowering my head, I said, "That's very nice of you to say. I guess I'll just go along with your program." Determined that I would humble myself to the process, I quickly stepped into line.

As I stood there putting on my apron, I tried to absorb her words and wrap my head around this whole thing. My heart was going to connect with another. OK, I'll just go with it. It just seemed so "out there." But looking at the people she had helped, I saw the proof of her success.

"Fred, sit down with me right over here." We settled into a booth and she said, "The first thing I want you to do is to tell me what your customers and colleagues meant to you—meeting them face to face or talking to them on the phone." Lisa always spoke with a smile on her face. Not a big, gaping toothy grin, just a pleasant expression. She radiated ease.

I thought for a second, and then said, "I really liked my customers. At least, most of them." And right then, I was suddenly at a loss for words. It had been so long, I had kind of forgotten exactly how I felt about them. Truth be told, I could remember only a handful of their names and faces, let alone explain what any of them meant to me.

"That's great, Fred." Lisa said, "but I can tell by your answer that they didn't mean that much at all." I felt like she had just smacked me on the side of my head. I was insulted. And before I could speak, she said, "I don't mean to be unkind, Fred, but you treated your customers as customers. But if you want to get back in the game, the key to connecting is this: Treat your customer as a person. And love the person that is your customer."

" And nobody really knows how it's done." Now, at that, I thought she had lost her mind. I was about to tell her that, back in the day, I had been very successful in sales and customer service. I had given talks on how to connect with people. I have been to seminars by the giants in the industry. And right when I was about to launch into my speech about how good I was, Lisa said, "Everybody thinks it's in the smile, the content of your delivery, and the inflection of your voice. That's only part of it, and that comes later." *I was thinking to myself, "Later?" How much later, if not right after 'Hi, my name's Fred?'"*

Just as I was about to open my mouth, Lisa said, "Before we go into further into the program, there's a couple of things that have to be understood, kind of a foundation of the techniques. Feel free to take notes. First, you have to make yourself available. Your affect and interpersonal energy, if you will, has to be inviting, safe, trustworthy, and friendly. In this spirit, you don't connect with people per se, *you let them connect with you.* By smiling, and by making yourself available, you're paying attention. By listening, looking in their eyes, and having a conversation, you begin to build trust. The whole concept of connection is built on trust. It's not about how well you make small talk. Anybody can say 'Hello.' Within the program that I'm going to teach you, it's the perspective you take, the attitude you assume and, subsequently, the connection you make."

"That may be true," I said, not even giving myself three seconds to absorb what she had just said, "but small talk helps break the ice. Isn't that what you do here?"

"No. That's not what I do here," she countered, as the smile disappeared from her face. "I open myself to people so that they feel they can open themselves a little to me. People will only be friendly if you're friendly. People will only be vulnerable if you're vulnerable. And people will only trust you if you're trustworthy. This is where the connection between two people truly takes place. By showing a little of your humanity, your fallibility, they are more comfortable showing their humanity to you." Lisa's eyes focused on mine as she said, "People expect so very little within the framework of any relationship. It makes this well worth the effort."

"When they are addressed by a human being instead of somebody who is only taking their order or trying to sell them something, people are truly taken aback. If a customer or a colleague feels that you are genuinely interested in them, whether you sell them anything or not, whether you serve them anything or not, they are going to remember your interest. They're going to remember that connection with you."

Paying close attention, but yearning to ask this question, I whispered, "Forgive me, but isn't the point of connecting with someone to master the art of the sale? Doesn't the relationship with the customer facilitate the buying process?" I remembered these things from, oh, years of sales and customer service. I thought this question was halfway intelligent, too.

Lisa smiled and looked at me as if she was about to pat me on the head, with a "there, there, you just don't know any better, do you?" expression on her face.

"Your connection has to be sincere," she said, "and it has to come from within you. And that connection has to come first. It precedes any exchange of goods or services. You really have to show the other person your heart, by being yourself. You don't just mouth the words."

"Maya Angelou said, "I've learned that people will forget what you said, people will forget what you did, but people will never forget how you made them feel." You should probably write that down. You'll learn to live by that quote."

She grabbed a pot of coffee and filled some cups on the counter. *I started following her as she continued to speak.* "There can be no pretense. Focus directly on them, who they are, and what you can do for them. Seems very basic, but this must be the first point of contact with another person."

Lisa turned and stood in front of me. "Let me back up a bit, because we're getting a little ahead of ourselves. Remember what I asked you to do when you first came into my place?" The first two points of the program lay the foundation for the next four."

I said that I didn't remember and politely asked her to tell me again what the two points were. She said, "We went through them kind of quickly, so thank you for asking me to repeat it." That made me feel good. Score one for me.

"But here's the first part that I really want you to pay attention to."

"I asked you to "Watch" and "Experience" your surroundings. That is how you should approach all situations with people, and this is key: When you first meet anyone, you need to take a second, just one second, to look at them-to "watch" everything about them, and then take in-or "experience," everything you're about to encounter."

She stopped for just a half second and stood right next to me. Looking straight ahead, she said, "When you "Watch" somebody, or "see" or "look" or even "observe" someone, you need to do two things, almost automatically. First, you take one deep breath. Not a really big ol' lung filler, just breath in and out." Then Lisa demonstrated. It was deep but didn't seem to take more than a half second. "It is in this moment that, after you relax just a little, you're better able to see that person. This breath helps you look at them with different eyes."

"Different eyes?" I said. I wasn't trying to be a wise guy, I honestly wasn't. I was trying to see if I heard her correctly. This wasn't exactly a term I'd ever learned in any business classes or trainings I'd ever attended.

"Yes," she said. "Think right now about somebody you really care about. Your grandmother, a parent, your child, your best friend, a sibling, a relative, maybe even your favorite pet. Within that breath, as a person approaches you, place them in the same category as somebody you truly care for."

Lisa paused, and said with calm deliberation, "It is, then, through these eyes, this focus from the heart, that you "watch" someone. You eliminate judgment; you withdraw predisposition. And you replace that with the feeling of kindness and attention you would give your best friend." I shifted my weight, and just kept my mouth shut. "Within those eyes, all that you see is another human being that deserves that same kind of patience, kindness, and respect that you would give to someone you deeply care about. All you see is another good soul that needs your focus and presence."

"Oh, and I should mention: Once you've arrived at this point, you'll likely be smiling."

"Then," Lisa continued," you "Experience." You're sitting back, becoming receptive to someone you're seeing as a loved one, somebody you deeply value. When they come to you, your first impulse won't be to evaluate or judge them. Instead, you "take in" the experience of them just being with you."

OK, this is where she began to lose me. I don't like the word, "experience," largely because it's just so vague. And I had no idea what "take in" meant, either. But I could tell she was about to explain this so, once again, I kept my mouth shut and paid attention.

"When you think of the word, "experience," think of how you "take in" a movie, you're "experiencing" the cinematic process, right? You bought your ticket, you're taking for granted the movie will be good, at least that's what you're anticipating, so you are ready to, as they say, "take in the movie." You're "watching" the movie as well as "experiencing" or "taking in" what it has to offer. "Experiencing" someone's presence, therefore, is to be fully present, to give someone your full attention."

Lisa continued, "Let's bring this into a more practical reality. If you go into a board-room meeting, take a second to look at your environment, to see the faces of the people around the table, to even look at the pictures. That's how you "watch." Stay with that and take one breath." I see Lisa inhale a deep breath, this time I noticed that it was right down to her abdomen. "In just a few seconds, that breath takes you into that environment, into your surroundings, to feel the place where you are standing. It plants you into the action and makes you present. You can see and feel where you are. You're "taking in" that movie, in this case the meeting, from the smell of the air to the feel of the floor, absorbing the ambiance, the energy, the vibrations, whatever you want to call it. You "watch" and then you "experience."

"Is that hard to quantify? Sometimes. But when you are truly experiencing something, from watching your child take his first steps to taking in the energy from another person, you're in that moment fully and completely. It takes a half second, but you're right there. You are with that experience, moment to moment, and the feeling you get is tangible. You know it when you've got it. And from that jumping-off point, you begin to establish your connection."

Once again, I'm trying to adjust my emotional bearings to all that she's just explained. Nobody—not one person, seminar, or book—has ever explained this to me in the way that she just had.

"Connection is actually the third step of this program, but I don't spend a great deal of time on it. Everybody, every single person, is skilled at connecting with another. In connecting with someone, you are only there to do one thing: Make their day better."

"OK," I said, "is there something I can do to make their day better? Are there a couple of things that I can focus on in order to facilitate that? I mean, each person is different, every situation presents a new challenge, so…" And right there, she interrupted me.

She said, "You make somebody's day better by being accepting, non-judgmental, and happy to see them."

She paused a second and said, "Anybody can carry on a conversation. But there always seems to be an unspoken, often ulterior motivation "Buy this, do this, facilitate that." Nobody is going to do anything for you if they feel you just want something from them. You have to engage that person first. You've heard this a million times, I'm sure, but few really do this."

Lisa straightened her back and said, "If someone feels that their day was improved a little because you crossed their path, you've done your job. You connected with them from the place in your heart that facilitates a relationship and establishes trust. That's how you know you connected, and that's how you know you were successful. That's the essence of interpersonal relationships and customer service."

"And now you know how to do that."

"Connection is what has made you successful. The only difference is that, this time, before you connect, you apply the "Watch" and "Experience."

Breathe, adjust your view and perspective, and then enjoy their presence."

I replayed these points in my head. Watch, Experience, and Connect. And as I tried to commit them to memory, I became instantly discouraged. She bases her connection on sharing that "place in your heart." Open my heart to another person? I'm not ready to be that exposed. I can carry on a distant professional relationship as well as anybody. But she's now talking about the value of sharing my insides with somebody else.

I could feel my anxiety rising, so I looked at Lisa and said, "I need to tell you this right away. If it's important be vulnerable and open to connect with another person, I'm not sure I do." Lisa looked at me as I continued, "The job that defined me, defined who I was, had changed years ago from salesperson to supervisor. And I was good at keeping that professional distance, very successfully playing both roles."

"But I have to go back to sales and customer service, and I am out of touch. My job is so vague right now that I'm not sure what my next step is supposed to be. And because of that, I'm not sure what you mean when you say to be yourself or, more importantly, to share my heart with another."

"You know, Fred, that's a fair statement." She grinned a little, looked away for a moment as if she was gathering her thoughts, looked back at me, and said, "Let me be clear on this: When you share yourself with another, your best posture is one of ease. Many people, when they begin this program, feel uncomfortable. They are seeing a new way of relating to people that they hadn't previously considered. They don't want to release their old ways of relating. They see some past success, and this may be all they have to grasp. In adopting this method, many not only feel that they won't be successful, they're afraid they won't be taken seriously by their peers and supervisors, and this creates some nervousness. This is completely understandable."

"The whole "Watch" and "Experience" thing helps take you out of that fear. It takes you outside of yourself and into the process of addressing the needs of another. Once you do it you'll feel much more comfortable in your own skin. You'll begin to trust your judgements, your instincts, and your assessments as you begin to trust being yourself."

"And I should explain what "being yourself" means. As I see it, being yourself means being genuine. It doesn't mean being on stage. It just means reaching the place where you are comfortable, and that comfort is demonstrated by the ease with which you share yourself with others."

"But that takes place," she said, "when you focus on someone else, and not yourself."

She saw I was confused and said, "I'll explain it even further. In my experience, people are most themselves when they feel accepted and when there is no fear or anxiety. For instance, when you are sitting with an older person who really appreciates your company, or a younger person who really needs your help. There will be no pretense, no ego, and certainly no anxiety in listening to the story of an elderly person while you look into their eyes and hold their hand. You are completely yourself in that moment. You're not there to impress, you're not there to show off— instead you're just there for them. Your presence or, more specifically, just being yourself, is good enough." She paused. "Same thing goes with a little kid. They're just looking for your attention. They just want you to be with them. So you do things without any fear and without much thought about how you'll be viewed. You play in the sand, you swing on the swings, and you listen to their story. In both situations, you suspend judgment on them and on yourself. In both situations, you're not there to make an impression. You're just there for the company, to offer a little bit of yourself to them."

"Using this attitude changes your perspective and how you interact with people, while offering you more insight into yourself. This is what "Watch and Experience" is based on. Your acceptance of the person in front of you, and your attitude of seeing them as somebody that you truly care for, takes your anxiety down a step. You're not judging them, you're accepting them for who they are. In that moment, that half of a second once you really dial it in, all of our negativity-anger and resentment, worry and fear, sadness and despair-begin to fade. And when you genuinely focus on the exchange between your heart and another, stepping straight into the premise of "Watch" and "Experience," those negative feelings take a backseat to the interaction at hand."

While I was trying to sort out everything I had just heard, Lisa interrupted my thoughts. "Remember "Watch" and "Experience" and practice that throughout your week. They lay the foundation. Then, add one more word: Connect. Think of what I just told you about how you connect with somebody. Watch, Experience, and Connect. Lead with your heart and the rest will follow."

Something still bothered me, and I just had to ask what seemed to be an obvious question. As I was leaving I said, "So, if you don't mind me asking, why a restaurant? Why not get a gig with a major corporate player out there?" I was curious how she was passed over by the corporate world. I figured she would have gotten more notice, and certainly more money, working as a Vice President of something or other somewhere to help interpersonal relationships within the corporate culture. I mean, she'd make bank doing this as a consultant. And yet, here she was with a book full of famous people in a restaurant on the corner of "the middle of nowhere," just down the street from "I'm not sure, but I think it's around here somewhere."

"Good question. Remember, my father was the head of a Fortune 500 firm. But understand this for a second. Say you've got an MBA, which I do, and your father's a big wheel, which he was. Do you think my chances of getting a Vice Presidency would be any better?"

"Well, yeah, absolutely," I said, and I meant it. How could anybody not see this woman's talent. And she's got the MBA which, I thought, was kind of cool. I suspected it after she said she'd had "graduate" studies, but still, and on top of that, a father that's connected?

"Well, let's put it this way: My father did help me get my first job and I was a manager at a young age. I started in Marketing and did a little Product Development along the way. But throughout, any promotion I sought was not mine to be had. My connections, if you must know, felt a little thin. I spent a great deal of my time at meetings listening and when I had something to say, I felt that my input was either minimized or, sometimes, flatly ignored."

"And," she said, grabbing a few things from the counter, "I didn't have any peers with whom to commiserate. I had no one with whom to compare notes. I thought, was it my age? My experience? My education? I was a woman? Maybe they didn't like my father?" Lisa stopped a second, and although she had her back to me, I could see her take a deep breath. She turned around, smiled, and said, "I don't mean to ramble, so I'll get to the point. Men communicated with me differently than they did with other men."

She took some things into the kitchen and kept talking. "It was right around that time I developed my Six Point Program. I felt that it could not only help with relationships with customers and colleagues, it would help my peers and me to actually speak to one another. I shared it with my boss, but nothing materialized."

Lisa leaned against the counter. "Then, not a week or so later, I overheard my boss working with a man who had his desk a few feet from mine. We had cubicles, but I distinctly heard him go through each point of the program with my coworker about how he could improve his communication by using my work. At that point, I confronted my boss and told him my work was copyrighted. He said he didn't see a problem and defended the coworker's use of my work. With that, I left the firm. I felt like a nobody, going nowhere. I felt completely invisible."

"And you know what?" she said, softening her voice but sharpening her focus, "My father didn't raise me to be invisible."

"So," she said, working a little around the front of the counter, "I remember the first job I ever had was as a waitress in a restaurant. I loved it. I loved the atmosphere and the way I interacted with people. I had enough money saved to put down a payment on this place, big enough to make some money but small enough to make some friends. And, at the same time, I told my father that I wanted to begin a small communication consultation business. I developed the protocol, and it was pretty formal at first. My father's friend and colleague referred my first client, and it has blossomed ever since."

"And do you know why I start my training with "Watch and Experience?" She was rolling now. I was humbled that she would share this much of her past with me, but I figured it was needed for me to fully understand her motives and her background into consultation. I said, "Well, yeah, OK. Why?"

"Because I never want anybody to make another person feel invisible again. Not one customer, not one peer, not anyone. We will turn this completely around. Not only will every person you see be perceived with a different attitude, you will see them with respect for the person they truly are."

"A worker that is happy is a productive worker. But a worker that feels understood, appreciated and truly listened to is a worker that is a trusted, productive, engaged, and an invaluable part of your process. If you see them through the attitude of "doing unto others as you would have done unto you," you are meeting them with your highest, best self. From that place," Lisa said, drawing a deep breath, "miracles happen. It is reflected in communication, interpersonal relationships, morale, customer relations and, most importantly, your bottom line."

"Well," she said, "I've spoken enough for one day. I think we're good." She put away her apron and got her keys to close up the restaurant. As I walked toward the door, Lisa said, "You're still wearing your apron." We both laughed a little, and Lisa said, "Fred, I know it was a lot today. Come on back next week, same day, and this time at your lunch hour and I'll tell you more about what we covered today. And make sure you tell me how you used what you've learned."

## CHAPTER SIX

Back at the office, my boss told me I had to take over a few accounts, and said, "we'll see what happens." Not exactly comforting. I could tell from his inflection that he wasn't overcome with confidence in me. Worries started racing around my head. Thoughts about sales, past successes, and things Lisa had said flew back and forth in my mind, and I didn't feel like I could get a handle on any of it. I sat at my desk for what seemed an eternity, trying to figure out what I needed to say or how I needed to say it. I had yet to pick up the phone to call my first account. And now, after not having sold anything or offered any customer service to anybody in years, I couldn't for the life of me think of what to do next.

I thought about what Lisa told me. I would try to connect with somebody. I looked at my stack of files and the record outlining each account, and my mind went blank. I sat back in my chair and looked across the office. At her desk across the room, I saw a woman I had supervised. I couldn't remember the last time I started any kind of conversation with her.

Her name was Charlene, and she had just had her birthday. I knew that because she still had a "Happy Birthday" balloon on her desk. How did I miss that? Was there cake in the lunchroom? Where was I? Anyway, as I looked at her desk, I saw a picture of a little girl, maybe about three. Had I not looked at her desk, I never would have known about the child, let alone known about her birthday. I realized how distant I'd become from the people in this office.

I was stuck. I didn't know what to say to anybody on the phone anymore and now, looking at Charlene, I wasn't even sure what to say to her. But remembering what I learned from Lisa, I dove right in. First, I took a second to "Watch and Experience." I paused for a second and took a breath.

Then, as I walked over to my colleague, I said, "Excuse me, Charlene?" I tried to sound friendly and get her attention. "Yes, Fred?" She looked directly at me, and she wasn't smiling. She was just waiting for me to say something but my mind was blank. All I could think of were the words I kept repeating at Lisa's restaurant hours before. I took that short but important breath, then kicked into the "Watch" mode. In a half second I could feel myself settling into the mental framework of "Experience" and I instantly became relaxed. Humbly, I said, "Is there anything I can get you?" And I sincerely meant it.

"I'm sorry, what did you say?" Charlene said, looking at me with a peculiar expression, like she was hearing this for the first time. And, when I took a second to think about it, she *was* hearing it for the first time. I'd never asked her that before. For that matter, I'd never asked any of my staff that question before. Pushing back my embarrassment, I said, "Well, what I mean is, is there anything that I can do for you? Could I be of assistance in any way?"

"No, Fred, thanks." That was it. That was all she said. And I was stuck. Couldn't think of a thing. "Watch," and "Experience" flashed through my head. I looked down, and out came the most profound thing I could think of saying:

"Oh, umm, well, OK."

What the….? I couldn't believe I had just said that. I had absolutely nothing to offer this woman. I also felt ashamed. I looked at the ground for a moment, my fingers flexing nervously. I didn't want to bother her but, frankly, I needed to connect with somebody. I wanted to know that I could still do it, that I still had it in me. And I wanted to follow through with what Lisa told me to do.

So I took a shot. Trying to get to "Experience," I was just trying to look at this woman with the same feelings I have when I look at one of my kids or some family member, maybe my aunt, my Mom, or my sister. After another breath I was able to alter my perspective and get to that place of ease again. Standing there for what seemed like an hour, I nervously said, "Charlene, is that a picture of your child on your desk?"

Charlene turned her head and looked at me with half a smile. "Yes, that's my daughter."

"What's her name?" Man, I felt sound so awkward.

"Her name is Jennie." Charlene looked back at the picture wistfully and said, "I took that picture in my mother's backyard. It was a beautiful day and Jennie was so happy."

"Do you get to see your mother often?" I immediately felt I got too personal. Maybe her Mom died? But I think Charlene was in her early thirties, so the odds were that she was still around for Charlene and her daughter.

Then I realized I was really over thinking every word I was saying. I also realized that this is exactly what happens when you don't know what to say and you're stuck finding any words that seem appropriate.

"No, she's about 200 miles away and I get there as often as I can. I really want Jennie to get to know her grandparents." A long silence followed. I didn't know what to say but I knew what I was feeling, so I just thought I'd lay it all out there. "Charlene, thanks for taking the time to tell me about your daughter." I wanted to express gratitude to her for carrying on a conversation with me. I didn't remember ever doing this when I was her boss.

"Fred," Charlene said, "I appreciate you even asking." She must have taken note of my embarrassed expression. She turned her chair toward me and said, "Fred, I know this must be hard for you. All of us in the department have been talking about how difficult it must be for you sitting at a desk with us, let alone getting back on the street." There was such kindness in her voice that I was at a loss for words. She continued, "How about this: If there's anything that I can do for *you*, just let me know. I'm happy to help in any way I can."

"Thank you, Charlene. Thank you so much. I truly appreciate that. I might just do that."

"You're welcome, Fred." She smiled, saying, "It's tough to get started but you'll do fine. Just do the things you've been telling us to do all these years." I couldn't remember what I'd been telling them all these years that did much good. I said, "I'll try. And thank you so much for the offer." Charlene grabbed her laptop bag, swung it over her shoulder, waved to me, and left.

I sat there, alone in the office, and thought about the first part of the program Lisa had shared: *Watch, Experience, Connect. Lead with your Heart and Be Yourself.*

And, looking back at my conversation, what Charlene just said to me was exactly that. She just demonstrated the ease of that entire process. She was relaxed, held no judgment, connected with me, and even left me with a word of encouragement. She expressed herself in a step by step format of how Lisa wanted me to use her program.

Then I wondered: Did I teach her that? Did she get that from me? Maybe she did, and I didn't even know it.

No, I didn't do any such thing. She's just a seasoned communicator that speaks like she's been trained by Lisa.

Hopefully, all this stuff I'm learning from Lisa will make me as good of a communicator as Charlene.

## CHAPTER SEVEN

A week passed and it was time for my next meeting with Lisa. Giving me an apron, Lisa said, "Fred, sit down at the counter for a minute. I want you to look around at all the people in this place right now. Let's go back to "Watch and Experience." Do that now, Fred." And I looked around. I set myself slightly, took a deep breath, and felt myself smile. That smile remained on my face as I took in every movement, sound, and feeling in the restaurant. Lisa said, "Watch and Experience for just a second. Bring yourself into this place and see what there is to see, feel what there is to feel. And, while you do that, I want you to think about this question: What is it that every one of these people has in common?"

I looked around the room and saw people eating their breakfast, drinking their coffee, and having conversations. They were reading the paper, working on their laptops, that sort of thing. And I was hard-pressed to think of anything that they had particularly in common. This was a diverse group.

So I asked Lisa if she could give me a hint. "I think I'm missing something. I'm not sure that I see what I'm supposed to be seeing and experiencing here." I said, feeling like I had just failed the test. Lisa smiled that trademark grin of hers and said, "It's OK. Look around the room again, and just tell me one thing that all of them have in common." Again, my mind went blank. I watched, just like she said, and I leaned into this experience, just like I was taking in a movie.

But I didn't come up with anything. Nothing seemed distinct. As I was looking around the room I heard myself say, "Well, they are all here."

"Exactly!" Lisa interjected. "That's it, Fred. They are all here. They are not eating their breakfast at home. They are not having their coffee in their car. They are in this restaurant. That's what they all have in common. And that is the lesson I'm going to teach you today. Last week I taught you some of the fundamentals: Watch, Experience, and then Connect with people. Today, you learn how to Assess when you're with another person—that's the fourth step in the program."

"Um, so, you want me to evaluate them?" I wasn't sure what she meant.

"No," Lisa said, "When you make an evaluation, you are drawing a conclusion and creating judgment. This separates you from the other person.

When you learn how to assess, through listening and observing, you're instead deepening your connection."

Lisa paused for a moment, turning her back to me. Looking around her restaurant, she said, "You see all these people, Fred? Policemen, firemen, salesmen, nurses, teachers, contractors, executives, truck drivers, and landscapers. And that's just the tip of the iceberg. They don't go to work thinking about how they can connect with people. They go to work thinking *about how they can help them.*

Their greatest function in life is assisting another person in need, whether it's laying a driveway, selling a product, mowing the lawn, taking a temperature, running a business, teaching a class, or driving a bus. Yeah, we want a paycheck. Of course we need to pay the bills. But the meaning in our work is to be in some scintilla of service to another. Every one of these people here has some measure of service within their job. And when you think about it, isn't that what we're here for? Isn't our purpose in life to consider the needs of others? Part of our humanness makes us able to assess these needs and offer our help when it is needed. All we have to do is identify the kind of assistance that will do the most good; that's the nature of an "Assessment."

"And it takes time," Lisa said. "You can't rush this. A good assessment demands focus, and more than a little patience. It keeps you with that person as long as necessary to truly get a sense of what they need. Assessing is observing, listening, and focusing.

She stopped for a moment, then said, "Oh, and one other thing: assessment includes the effective and meaningful use of one question:

"How can I help you?"

This time, I took out a little notepad and started writing. assessing is observing and listening, and one question." When I looked up at Lisa, her face wore the expression of understanding I'd become used to seeing.

As I opened my mouth to ask her to explain, she raised her index finger to stop me from speaking, and said, "When I stand at the table, with my order book and pen in hand, and I say the words 'How can I help you?' I mean it. It isn't just a throwaway line to begin the conversation. It comes from my heart. It elicits the information that I need to help someone. It is the fundamental sentence of assessment."

"And then I listen. I listen to what I'm being told, not to the voice in my head preparing what I want to say. I have confidence in myself enough to know that, when the time comes to speak, I'll know the right words. So when my customers are speaking, I listen in order to assess."

Lisa paused and said, "Very few people truly listen. Most are thinking about what they will say when the other person stops talking."

"Yeah, I know," I said. "But don't we all do that in some measure?"

"I'll be honest," Lisa said, "I did many years ago. I realized that every time my thoughts went to a response, I wasn't listening. So when a thought comes in my head, I realize I'm thinking and not listening, and I refocus on the person who is speaking. Over time, it's become pretty reflexive."

I sat there and paid attention. My head was swimming with things to remember. As soon as the questions started popping up, I thought about the "fundamental sentence of assessment." I asked, "You're talking about assessing their needs, right? And this follows connecting with your customer. But then you told me about being myself. But I have to ask: Aren't I providing a service? Isn't it just that simple? I mean, you're talking about this emotional dance between me and the customer, and I really don't think it's that deep."

I was just being honest, and it felt good, so I continued. "I know these people come to see you. They can get food anywhere. And although what you provide is good, I get that they like the service and they really like you."

Lisa raised her eyebrows slightly, and said, "What we're talking about here is allowing somebody to know and experience your essence. Yes, you have to Watch, Experience, Connect, and Assess their needs. But in this part of the process, while you're offering your assessment, you have to be visible. They have to see *you*. They need to know who you are. And when you say, 'May I help you?' you have to put yourself out there. You offer somebody the opportunity to accept your gift of assistance, of kindness, with gratitude. It makes them feel better. They appreciate it. And it brings them closer to you."

Now, at this point, I was taking all the mental notes I could muster. Lisa looked at the clock and said, "I have to get back to work. But here's your homework: You go back to your office and assess the needs of one of your coworkers or clients. Listen, connect as best you can, and put yourself out there. Then report back to me in a week, at lunchtime."

## CHAPTER EIGHT

At the office, I was not exactly encouraged. I looked at my silent phone (which I'd been doing way too much of lately), and sat back in my chair, wondering about my next move. I thought about this whole assess thing but, again, I was stuck.

As I was about to pick up the phone and dial the number of some unknown customer in some far-away place, I heard a male voice behind me say, "Fred, do you have a minute?" It was Dave, a customer service representative who was new to sales. He had been around for about the last six months. Usually eager to please and anxious to learn, today the expression on his face was one of worry and doubt.

I told him I'd be happy to talk to him, and he pulled up a chair and sat down. He was trying to close a sale, he told me, but he was having difficulty meeting the customer's request. After listening to a rather involved explanation outlining all he did and said to all the parties involved, I thought about what Lisa had told me. Having just returned from meeting with her, here I sat with an opportunity to hear and assess this young man's dilemma.

I began to focus on what he was saying, but also on how he was saying it. I listened to the words, inflection, and emphasis he gave to each concern. I consciously worked to keep myself from drawing a conclusion. I wanted to hear what he had to say, so I focused not on my own thoughts but, instead, zeroed in on the details of Dave's predicament. It was hard to put aside my urgent sense that I should fix this problem. And a quick fix was not what I had learned from my new mentor just an hour before. "I am here to help," I thought, "I am here to listen. I am here to focus on Dave."

Once Dave was finished speaking, I said, "Well, Dave, I'm here to help you any way I can." And then, with a pause, I said, "What can I do to help you make this better?" That's the sentence that came straight from my heart. It sounded like somebody else was saying it, but I meant what I said. I wanted to make this better for Dave. I had been in his shoes one hundred times at his age and I had wished somebody had been there for me, to put things right, to give me a direction. It was curious that I hadn't really done this for him when I was his supervisor. But now, here I was, fresh out of a lesson from Lisa, doing what I should have done all along.

Dave and I tossed around some ideas and his next moves became clearer to him. He came by later in the afternoon and thanked me for my help, to which I said, "I'm not sure I really made much of a difference, but you're totally welcome." Not trying to be self-depricating, just being honest. Dave turned his head and said, "No, Fred. I really appreciate you listening, you know, just caring about what I had going on. Thanks for that. Thanks for caring."

There's that word. Lisa said it in our first meeting: Care. I'm not sure that I had expressed a great deal of that during my time as a supervisor. And I'm almost positive I didn't do my best to express any of it to my customers.

After Dave left, I turned and sat in front of my desk. It was time. I sent an email blast to all my customers. Now I have to follow it up. There's the phone, right in front of me. And I'm thinking, "Gotta get back into the game. Make a call. Make something happen."

I picked up the phone and dialed the number for the first person on my list. He was an old customer who I hadn't spoken to in quite a while. From my recollection, it could have been anywhere from several months to a couple of years. I needed to say something to reintroduce myself to this person who had always been part of an active account, always a steady customer. I needed to begin this relationship again. Right at that moment, though, I knew that there wasn't much I could sell this person, and there wasn't a clear service I could provide.

He answered the phone, and when the threads of our informal banter began to thin, I said, "You know, today I really called with one purpose in mind: To let you know that I want to be of assistance. I want to help in whatever way I can." I paused a moment to take a breath, and said, "Truth be told, I could use your help as well." The customer was a little taken aback, I could tell from the silence. For a second I wished I hadn't said those words, but I continued, "I want you to help me understand your needs. And I'm here to listen. I'm here to respond to you in a way that makes a difference. And if I don't get a sale because my service is substandard, that's okay. I mean that sincerely. But if I know more about you, your business, your needs, and the difficulties you have on your end, I can better serve you."

I meant it. I could feel it. It wasn't lines out of the latest "Caring for your Customer" seminar.

Something in my words felt differently.

Again, there was silence on the other end. I felt I had really overplayed my hand. Then he said, "Well, Fred, you gave me a lot to think about. I'm about to pour myself a cup of coffee right now. Let me roll this over in my head for a bit."

Then I said something that changed the nature of our relationship forever. I said "Coffee. You drink coffee?" OK, so it's not the brightest question I could have asked. Thankfully, the customer said, "You know, sometimes I'm not really sure. The stuff that they make around here doesn't taste like much, but it's strong, it's warm, and it's in a pot that says, 'coffee.' So, I guess that's what it is." Thinking about Lisa, I said, "Well, there's this stuff

I get from across the street. The guy roasts his own beans. One of the best cups of coffee I've ever had. How about I bring you over a pound?"

Taken off guard, he said, "No, Fred, that's not necessary. Besides, I don't know if I'm going to be here today." I recognized that he wanted to introduce some distance, so I said, "Well, that's okay. I'm going to get a pound and drop it off for you. But tomorrow morning, try that coffee out."

About an hour later I dropped off a pound of coffee, as I said I would. The next day, I called this customer, cup of coffee in hand, to listen and assess the ways that I could be of service. I made a note to myself to tell Lisa the next time I was in the restaurant. I decided to do this with as many customers as I could. I like having coffee with people, even if it's over the phone. Once in a while, if they turn on FaceTime or Skype, maybe we could at least see each other, or actually sit down across a table with them in person. And, as these folks made themselves available to me, I could begin to know each of them a little more, over that cup of coffee. In this way I could find out about them, their needs, and, more importantly, a little more about who they really were and what I could do to help each one of them.

I was learning to assess again. I was becoming a better listener. And, as a result, I was responding to my customer's needs. I was connecting with my client as a person and treating him as I'd like to be treated. And my initial skepticism of Lisa and her methods was beginning to fade. I made a note to myself to let her know how much she had helped me out.

## CHAPTER NINE

I did pretty well over the next week, and I made a couple of appointments to have coffee with my customers, some in person, but mostly on the phone. Although I was reacquainting myself with the process of customer service, assessing their needs and responding accordingly, I was discovering that one thing hit me hard, harder than it used to. Several of my customers were very difficult. In fact, a few of them were downright rude. Although almost two-thirds of the people took me up on my offer of a cup of coffee, when I met with them or spoke to them on the phone, several people let me know that what I did, and what my company did wasn't good enough, that we didn't afford them the kind of service they were looking for, and that they expected me to make a lot of corrections and improvements, immediately.

I tried to take all their collective input and listen attentively. I evaluated the merit of their complaints and assessed the nature of their concerns. I recognized that not every product is a perfect fit, and not every service can address every person's needs. But when I had coffee with them, I had anticipated being met with a little more friendliness. I mean, after all, they did take me up on the coffee. I thought that was great, and I figured we could just pick up where we left off, maybe tweak a few things about the business. And presto, a new relationship would be off and running.

Truth be told, that actually happened in several, if not most, of the meetings that took place. But I'd say about one in five had a major concern that they needed to get off their chest.

I came away from some of these meetings not knowing whether my assessment skills were any good, if I was missing something, or if I was just a little rusty on the engagement process.

Later that same day, around lunchtime, I had another appointment with Lisa. I really didn't feel like putting on the apron and pouring coffee, and I was hoping that I could just sit her down and run a few of these thoughts past her.

"Hi, Fred, grab an apron." Ugh. I really wanted to talk to her today. So I caught her eye and very quickly said, "Will you have a few minutes to talk at the end of the shift?" She said, "Maybe. But here's your assignment: Your job today is to wait on those two tables in the corner." She pointed first to a table with a man and a woman, and next to it was another table with four large men.

"You wait on them completely. They both just came in and sat down. After they leave, you and I can talk. But your lesson today will come from those two tables."

I went over to the couple at the first table and asked them what they'd like to drink. The woman, in her late 60s if she was a day, said, "I'd like herbal tea. Do you have any peach-cinnamon decaf?" I told her

I wasn't sure, but that I could go check, and then the man who appeared to be her husband said, "Well, before you go check on her, give me a cup of coffee." I smiled politely and said I'd get right on that. They seemed a little particular, but it was nothing too terrible.

Then I stopped at the table with the four large men. Each one was the size of a small dump truck. You couldn't park any of these guys in your driveway.

"Nice skirt," said the first guy as I walked over to the table. When I tried to take their drink orders, another guy, his neck disappearing into his chest, said, "Coffee and water for all of us, Honey." And they all broke out in laughter.

For the next 25 minutes, I was juggling between these two tables. To begin with, nothing was right at the first table. Her water was too hot, the tea was too weak, and the toast was too brown. The man was just as crabby. Nothing came fast enough for him. He even complained that the portions were too large. "How do you expect me to eat all this food?" I just smiled and went to the table with the guys who had all tied for the "guys with the biggest waistlines in the restaurant" contest. As I filled their coffee cups, the teasing was pretty harsh. And when they got up to leave, a couple of them said, "Thanks for the service, sweetheart." One guy even winked at me and blew me a kiss.

I looked over to Lisa, and she was standing at the end of the counter, smiling. It almost felt like I had been set up. Trying to cover a little smirk, Lisa finally said, "So, how did you like those customers this morning?" While she was making change at the register, I said straight out, "What was your point with this exercise?"

"I think you know exactly what my point was." Lisa closed the cash register drawer, looked me square in the eye, and said, "These are the customers that you are going to be dealing with for the rest of your career. These are the twenty percent of the 80/20 rule, if you know what I'm talking about."

I knew exactly what she was talking about. Twenty percent of your clients take up eighty percent of your time. This has been an adage in sales and customer service since, well, forever. Lisa said, "These are the customers that bring out our best. Without these customers, we would get lazy and slip into an unproductive routine." Lisa looked at me and said, "I'm sure you know what I'm referring to. Right, Fred?"

I had to bite my tongue a little bit. She was right.

Lisa said, "I put you over there to see what you had. I've been watching you serve these customers over the last half hour. And you did a pretty darn good job of staying connected, of assessing their needs, and treating them like you'd want to be treated. You were good."

"But," she said, "You also did something I don't think you realized. You didn't react from the impatience you were feeling or the frustration that came up. You responded with kindness and ease. I was impressed."

I was grateful for the recognition and praise. I figured Lisa had previous experience with these customers, so I blurted out a dumb question: "You know these people?"

Lisa looked at me and said, "Of course I know them. They've been coming here for about fifteen years. And they are like that every time they sit down."

Somewhat stunned that she had been letting these annoying people come to her restaurant for a decade and a half, I said, "And they have never gotten on your nerves?"

"Of course they get on my nerves. Every single time they're here. They are part of my twenty percent. And I treat them as well, sometimes even better, than the customers I truly enjoy."

I couldn't believe it. "You must be one of the most patient people on the planet," I said.

"No. But I have learned the proper way to respond. I don't react. I don't ever engage in the old adage, 'Fire, Aim, Ready.'"

I liked that one. I wrote it down in my notebook.

"Look," she said, "through connecting and assessing, responding to the customer gets easier. Responding will become your natural communication, thanks to your sincere connection and mindful assessment," Lisa praised. "You've quickly taken to the first four points of this training."

"But, let me digress a little bit," Lisa enthused. "The staff and I have an alert code when a customer or group of difficult customers needs to be served. We take turns because serving them can be a little draining."

"An alert code?" I asked.

"Yes, the code is CM. I whisper 'CM' and the table number into the ear of one of my staff so they can shore up their patience when they respond to the customers' needs."

Curious, I said, "OK, I'm game. What does CM stand for?"

Lisa leaned in and whispered in my ear, "Concrete Marshmallows." I couldn't wait to hear what she meant.

Lisa put her hand on the counter and, speaking in a somewhat quieter tone said, "Look, you've been doing this sales and customer service job for a long time, and so have I. You're not Mahatma Gandhi and I'm not Eleanor Roosevelt. " We both laughed a little. She continued, "These are the customers that we use to gauge our success. It is through our responsiveness to these people that we really earn our money. And it is through them that we keep ourselves in check."

"They're not bad people. I don't believe that any person is bad. I think inherently, we're all good. We are all born with the same spirit, the same soul, and the same need for love. These people, to me, are in particular need of love from us. They may not always show the best sides of themselves. They may not know how. We see the tougher side, the side that meets the world every day; that's the "concrete." So it is up to us to show them the best side of ourselves, to connect with them any way we can, so they can feel more at ease, a little less guarded, and a little less defensive. We have to redouble our kindness. We have to offer them light to brighten whatever darkness they may be feeling. When we do that, we bring out that inside, the sentimental, good spirit we all have within us. That's where the marshmallow lives."

I said, "Doubling the effort of kindness. Do I have that straight?"

"No, you misunderstood." Lisa said, "It's re-doubling. That means *four* times the effort you would ordinarily make. You'll see and feel yourself really trying to connect. Trust me, these folks require it."

Lisa looked at me. " Watch, Experience, Connect and Assess…I tell you, with these folks, you really need to use all four. And you add one more, which is what I wanted to see in you today."

"What?" I said. I didn't understand what she just said. "I'm sorry, what did you want to see in me?"

"The way you responded. That's the next lesson. Respond. I told you that I never react? Well, you'd have to ask my employees how they see me, but I think I've gotten past reactivity. With as many people as I can, I respond to their needs."

"With the Concrete Marshmallows' I lean in a little more. That is, I try to be a little more inquiring, a little more interested. I bring "assess" right to the front, then I respond right after. And, I do both with compassion. I take the attitude that being a CM is a result of unhappiness. They just need a little more attention, a little more love, that's all. But you have to prepare yourself every day to respond, not react, to folks like this, and it's so much more than just giving them a nickname. It requires setting your own ego aside and realize their temperament and demeanor is part of who they are; it has absolutely nothing to do with you."

"But," I said, "doesn't this wear on you? I mean, while waiting on people in a restaurant, particularly if you're a woman, *don't* you come across all kinds of dismissing, demeaning and insulting statements from people?"

"And," I said, "have any of these guys been inappropriate? You're a woman. All your waitresses are women. How do you deal with them? I mean, a waitress is ground zero for sexual harassment. "More attention, more love" couldn't be your response here."

I then asked, "I was wondering what you'd do if you felt your boundaries were severely violated. If you were harassed, approached, touched in an inappropriate manner…"

"Well," Lisa said very deliberately. She leaned against the counter and said, "I'll be brief on this. I run this place now, but for years I worked here as a waitress. I had to endure the hassle, the harassment, and the pressure of having to attend to the needs of men that treated me and the other waitresses in this place with chronic disrespect. They weren't many. But we knew who they were."

"I was told things that I won't repeat. Things about my appearance, my look, and how much "fun" they'd have with me. I'd take their order, smile, and just play along. I'd bring them their order, and they'd do the same again. This went on for years."

"So how did you handle it?" I said.

"I tolerated it," she said, "because I felt it was necessary. Building a reputation as a good restaurant takes years. Within that time, you build up a customer base. You offer the best service, best food, best prices. But I compromised when it came to that kind of treatment. I was afraid that if I stood up for myself, I wouldn't keep their business. I feel badly about that. I should have been stronger. I put up with it for too long. But I don't anymore." She paused a second and said, "You know what? That's not exactly true. It's more like this. I make sure that anyone who begins down that road with me or any of my staff knows right away, in a gentle but firm manner, that this isn't acceptable behavior, and I expect more from good men like themselves. It sets the appropriate limit, but kindly."

"And mind you, I only have to deal with these guys in spurts. Little bits of contact. Take the order, go. Drop the plates, go. I didn't have to stand there for a long period of time." She took a second to look around the room. "You move from place to place. However," she said, pointing her finger at me, "in most businesses, women are stuck. Women are held captive. They have had to tow the line with unfairness since time immemorial. Lower wages, next to zero opportunities for advancement, and treated in an inferior, substandard manner. Harassment, predatory behavior has been the norm."

"But no more," she said, "and the training I'm giving you is going to put an end to it."

I wasn't sure I heard this correctly. "This training is going to stop harassment?," I said, and shut up immediately.

"More than that," she said, quickly. "It will bring women to the table again. You will no longer look at them as objects. The perception of being "less than" or "different" from you will disappear. This training helps men look at women as equals. You remember "Watch," and "Experience," right?

"Yes," I said, then shut my mouth. I wanted to make sure I didn't get in the way of her message.

"Well," she said, "I need to draw this out just a little bit, so bear with me. To "watch" and "experience in this or, for that matter, any other context a man has an encounter with a woman, it means, "I am watching this woman with the eyes of a brother, a father, an uncle, a son, a nephew, a grandson and a grandfather. I am "experiencing" their presence as one that I have a feeling of family, of brotherhood. This kind of attention and response fits into two kinds of definitions. They come from the Greek; one is "Storge" and the other is "Philia," friendship within a family, friendship among your friends."

"And you know what?" she said, stopping and standing still. "I need to make this point. It's not meant to be unkind, it's just something that you should know. I have never had to spend more than a minute with a woman on this concept. They get it right away. Men, on the other hand, need to be reminded continually. Most of the men have a much harder time. I always have to run this message throughout the training by phrasing their approach with, "Would you want your wife/mother/sister/daughter treated this way? *If you witnessed this, how would you respond?"* I usually lay that foundation in the first session, particularly if somebody is coming to see me because of harassment or inappropriate behavior with woman. I don't try to shame them into compliance, not at all. I want to make sure I'm clear about that. Instead, I just want to change their perspective. I want them to look at a woman through the eyes of friendship and family. From there, it becomes a habit."

"I'll tell you something else you probably didn't realize: For every woman I've trained, I've trained ten men. Maybe more than that. That's ninety percent of the training I've done is to help men communicate in a lighter, easier and relaxed fashion."

I kept listening. "And I'll say one last thing about this. A wise woman who works in Silicon Valley said that sexual harassment will stop when women get into positions of power. She's right. But until then, when men use this mechanism, the whole landscape of attitude and communication between men and women will change." She put down her water glass and said, "From this point of understanding and respect, women will finally be treated *and spoken to* fairly and professionally. Every woman, in every situation, no matter who they are, where they're from, or how they look. If they can do the job, they are treated and spoken to like an equal. This mechanism guarantees that."

"And know this: When you prepare yourself for your job, you have to make sure that you are emotionally equipped to handle whatever comes your way. You have to be sure that your balance has been steadied. It guarantees that your response will be calmer and more at ease. The six points, of which you've learned four, will help you do that, too. And now here's your fifth point: Respond."

"You mentioned that earlier. I wrote it down."

"Good. Glad you were paying attention." She started to move to the other side of the restaurant to clean off a table. "To respond well," Lisa said, "you obviously want to keep yourself calm, and that just takes a little practice. Everybody wants this, but few know how to do it. You want to make sure that what you're bringing to the table every day is your absolute best. But it's not the kind of "best" that you're thinking. Use the points so far: Watch, Experience, Connect, Assess, and especially Respond, and you'll surprise yourself at how well you're doing. I mean, let's face it. People like this will test you day in and day out, for the duration of your career. And keeping yourself as calm and centered is the centerpiece to this last point. Therefore, to be successful, you have to prepare yourself every day to respond."

My brain caught on that word, "prepare." "So," I said, "if you don't mind me asking, what do you do to prepare yourself every morning?" I figured she must have perfected a complex ritual to arrive at the place of balance, that calm demeanor. And I really wanted to know what she did.

I was a little surprised when she said, "I pray and meditate." She paused for a second. "I haven't been in a church in a long time, but I begin my day by taking ten minutes to pray and ten minutes to meditate." She continued, "I take ten minutes to thank God and ask for guidance, and another ten minutes to clear my mind, to just sit and concentrate on my breathing. Sometimes, I try to listen to what God might have in mind for me, but I meditate in a pretty classic fashion, I guess, both activities center me. Both prepare me. And both do more for my overall mental and emotional balance than I can begin to explain. A sense of faith and an ability to meditate have been shown time and time again to quell anxiety, depression, and anger. I just don't understand why more people don't take the time to do this every day."

Having never meditated nor been someone who prayed much about anything, I was hesitant to ask her how I should begin, so I asked with a tone of caution in my voice. I told her I never learned how to meditate and prayed very little, then asked her how I should begin learning and applying both.

"This is something that I think you should find on your own, but I highly recommend you learn how to meditate. You don't have to do it for very long. Ten minutes in the morning helps me a great deal. I learned it from a book, "The Journey Within," by Ruth Fischel. I have to put aside that time each day."

"As far as prayer goes, I've prayed since I was a little girl. I know that, in most spiritual texts, there's something along the lines of "ask and you shall receive" in all of them. But I don't ask for much. These days, I borrow a prayer from Father Greg Boyle: "Resting in you, resting in me." I just want to have a relationship with God, whomever or however you recognize that spirit. And I always end my prayer time with the best prayer you can offer: "Thank you." Start your day with meditation and gratitude and it will help you a great deal. Work on putting aside twenty minutes each day, preferably in the morning after you've had your coffee, when you can draw that practice into your routine."

I thanked her and she said, "We covered a ton today. I'll speak to you a little more about "respond" the next time we see one another." I thanked her and walked to the door.

"And," she said, "If you run into any Concrete Marshmallows this week, I want to hear about how you handled them!"

## CHAPTER TEN

This week was slow. I was on the phone trying to reconnect with old clients but meetings, mostly about the disappointing quarterly sales numbers, came up three times in five days. That, plus the installation of a new computer system, took up nearly all of my time. While I'm seeing my staff-now my peers-taking off to see different accounts, I was stuck in the office tying to establish any kinds of leads I could. I looked at the calendar, saw that I was almost late for an appointment with Lisa, so I checked out and headed over to the restaurant.

Instead of handing me an apron, Lisa poured a couple of iced teas, and we sat on stools at the counter. She turned to me, and said, "So, today I'm interested in hearing from you about our training. Anything you'd like to talk about before I get started?

I played with my tea for a second and said, "It was a slow week. Maddening, actually. I didn't visit one client and the calls seemed deliberate. The clients on the other end of the phone were more terse, to the point, and impatient. But I didn't change a thing in my approach."

"Well," I said, "that's not altogether true. I put a stronger emphasis on my ability to respond. I mean, that was tough. Keeping my focus on them as a person instead of being effected by and attached to their anger was hard. And sitting in meetings having to deal with the same old stuff was really testing my patience. But I focused on your formula, particularly on the "response" part if it.

Lisa paused for a second, somewhat deliberately, and said "That was good. And given that success through the stress, this might be a good time to expand on that."

I listened as Lisa said. "You intuitively responded to the week's stresses correctly, but I'm going to tell you what you did, so you know how to do it again the next time something like this comes up. I've already talked to you about *watch* and *experience*, how to *connect* with somebody. Then, we talked about how to *assess* their issues. We got to how to *respond,* which we covered a little the last time. But before I elaborate on that, I want to tell you about the opposite of responding."

"The opposite of responding? Like, reacting?"

"Yes." Lisa took a sip from her glass of iced tea sitting on the counter and said, "The opposite of respond is *react*. You can be a first-class connector. You can be the absolute best at being able to assess any variety of issues. But if you react, everything preceding it goes out the window."

"Now," Lisa said, "this may sound a little remedial, but I need to bring this forth so you can put this into the process I'm teaching you."

"I'll be patient. I won't react." Lisa smiled. I thought it was pretty good, actually.

"If," she said, "you react in the beginning or within the introduction of the issue or encounter, you immediately lose the connection. These folks will no longer give your counsel much meaning or your assessment much thought if you are reactive. It diminishes everything about your message, and it calls into question your ability to manage relationships and people— let alone provide good service— in any personal encounter."

"Here's an example, let's say that someone, either an employee or customer, has presented you with a concern. You have a relationship with this person that's pretty strong. It's been established over time, maybe over a few years. You know them, they know you, and they've been through this with you before. Then, as they present their information, you assess the nature of their concern. You're thinking about the details, you're evaluating the nature and the scope of the issue. But then," Lisa stopped for a second, in a deliberate pause, and said, "You interrupt. You jump in before they are done explaining their issue. You speak quickly. Your demeanor conveys urgency."

"Now you tell me," she said, "how you think that person is going to respond to you? Even if what you say is spot-on, and your solution is absolutely the right thing for this person to do, how much confidence will they have in you? And, regardless of your friendship, how do you think they're going to feel, leaving that discussion?"

"Well," I said, "I guess they might feel a little dismissed. They would have the feeling that either I had something better I needed to do, or that I knew the answer and wanted to hurry the process. Or maybe that I didn't think their problem was that important?"

Lisa nodded her head and said, "Correct on all counts."

She quickly added, "To respond, though, you prepare the same way you did to assess the issue. You prepare yourself to stay as calm and relaxed as you can. Responding appropriately merits careful attention and awareness. But it has to become part of you. It's like breathing."

"Here's another tip. Think of somebody who makes you feel really good. Think of somebody who makes you feel loved, relaxed, and comfortable. Get that image in your crosshairs. Keep that with you. If it's available to you, put a picture of that person up on your desk. You want to access the goodness of that person. You want to make sure you can emulate their same spirit of giving in your encounters with every person you have sitting in front of you or on the other end of the phone. Some people cite a teacher, a friend, a grandparent, or their mother or father as someone who made them feel loved, appreciated, special, and important. I've had people who placed a poem, a picture of a treasured place, or lyrics to a song in a frame that offered them the same feeling. You want to convey this sentiment, in a calm and loving fashion, in every encounter that you have. This is the foundation of how you respond, and it comes as a result of the first four points."

Then Lisa paused a moment. "Fred, let me take a step back a second. This is another foundational issue, but it's the big thing you want to communicate in your response."

"And that would be?" I asked, curiously.

Lisa said, with great verve and emphasis, "It's Love. L-O-V-E." Lisa leaned in a little and said, "I have always felt that if you can't love them, you can't help them. If you can't love them, if there isn't even a little bit of love in the air through your ability to connect, your ability to assess, and your ability to respond, they will know. They'll feel it. Trust me on this. If you love somebody, it's in the air, and it can be heard within every syllable. It's the feeling behind your words."

"People shy away from that word, absolutely run in the other direction when they hear it within the context of any business or professional relationship, and I understand some of the reasons. Even mentioning the word can make some people really uncomfortable."

"And yet it underscores every valued human connection, every interpersonal exchange, every friendship, every overture of kindness. Love is the start of all the meaning and purpose life has to offer. Love is why we're here. Love is what we are meant to do. Love is what gives us direction, faith, hope, and motivation. It is the emotion that sustains us, is the spirit that gives us life. Love is that on which we stand. I told you about Philia and Storge? That's it, right there."

Lisa's tone and volume softened, but her emphasis remained strong. "Without it, we are lost. We lose our direction and our mooring. Love is the energy that knits us together. It is our best self. It is the reason that we are good, the reason that we try, the reason we connect, and the reason that life matters. Love is the foundation—and never underestimate its power. A glance, a touch, a smile, a gesture, an expression of kindness: these can change the way a person feels from that moment, that day, that week, into the rest of time. How we exchange our love with another person is really how we gauge all our responses. You've got to hear me when I'm telling you this, Fred: If you're going to get good at this, it's because you love the people you're dealing with, no matter their response, no matter how challenging they can be."

"You have to express love in a tangible, consistent, meaningful manner in order for your life to matter to you again. And, for your life to matter to somebody else."

"…and, for your life to matter to somebody else." That hit me like a brick. Her words resonated deep within me. I needed my life to matter again, both to me and to someone else.

Lisa turned and said, "Know this: Love has form. The form I've already explained is the kind that needs expression within the corporate culture: Respect, Friendship, and Family. This will be the difference in your communications with every person in your professional life."

I said goodbye to Lisa and she told me she'd see me next week. Three hours had gone by since I walked into the door.

And as I got into my car, I felt distinctly different.

## CHAPTER ELEVEN

A few days had passed. I thought I was connecting well with my clients and co-workers. My assessments and my responses both improved. I was listening well, and I understood their concerns with more ease than I had in the past. And I was responding to these concerns from my heart. I was treating each person as, well, a person. I was looking at them in a different way. I was offering them the same kind of empathy, consideration, and love in my heart that I would any friend or family member.

My sales were beginning to pick up, and I had not received one complaint from any of the people I served. In fact, I was receiving more consistently positive feedback than ever before. I could feel things begin to turn around.

Then I remembered Lisa had said that she was going to teach me six things. I counted five. She asked me to "Watch" and "Experience" before I engaged a situation. She taught me how to "Connect" more effectively; she taught me how to "Assess" through effective listening, and she taught me how to "Respond" with a patient and measured approach. I looked at my calendar and realized I was meeting Lisa later today.

When I arrived at the restaurant, Lisa greeted me immediately with, "Hey Fred, I just wanted to tell you how great you've been doing this week."

Usually when we first meet, she says "hello" and then gives some directions, or asks a question or two, that sort of thing. But since she didn't say any of that, I said hesitantly, "Uh, thanks."

And just before I could say something else, she said again, "You know, you've really done a great job these last few weeks. Thank you so much for taking to heart this whole process. You will be up to speed with this format in no time."

Then she went about setting a couple of tables. She didn't even make eye contact.

Again I thanked her, and when she was done setting the table, she launched into, "And I'm sure that with the talent you've displayed, you are going to…"

I cut her off. I raised my hand, looked away from her for a moment, and then said, "Hold on, hold on. I appreciate the praise, but can you explain why you're doing this?" I didn't want to sound defensive. I just wanted to know why all the compliments, and why did it seem so out of context? It was the first thing she said when I walked into the restaurant. It took me off guard.

Lisa smiled, came over to me, put her hand on my shoulder, and said, "Fred, what was I doing just now?"

"Praising me? Pumping me up?" I said, not sure of the answer, but thinking I was probably in the ballpark.

"I was offering you encouragement. Granted, it wasn't the best or most thoughtful way to encourage you, but I was trying to get your attention. And I was trying to make a point."

"Huh?" That was all I could say. I was trying to wrap my mind around what she just said, but I had about three things going on in my head. Even though I couldn't focus on any of them, I figured I should say something. And "huh" was what I came up with. OK, it wasn't my best comeback.

"Fred, there are two kinds of encouragement: Connected and Disconnected. The kind of encouragement I just gave you had no context. You came in and there was no connection between the two of us whatsoever. They're words. I gave you bumper sticker phrases that anybody can throw out."

"Encouragement is fundamental to any communication with every staff member, client, or peer. You have to encourage them and let them know they're doing a good job, that you are thankful that they are with you, that you appreciate who they are and what they have offered you. And, most importantly, you have to let them know through your encouragement that you believe in them. Encouragement ties everything together."

"But, you see," Lisa paused for a moment, "you have to have a connection in order for encouragement to stick. You have to have a supportive, engaged relationship with that person for any kind of praise or support to matter. Otherwise, it's just a drive-by comment. There is no thought or feeling behind it. The words will not be absorbed. Worse, you will sound disingenuous. True encouragement is specific and reflects an understanding of both the situation and the individual."

She had absolutely made her point. When I walked in, I had thought she was from another planet. She was throwing these words of praise at me and I was feeling absolutely nothing. I had to hand it to her; this woman knew what she was doing. And now I had learned the final step in the program: Encourage.

She continued, "Encouragement isn't a vehicle, either. You can't put it into a format, and I'll give you an example: "The Praise Sandwich." It's disguising criticism between two statements of praise; criticism negates the praise altogether. There's no encouragement, no support. It's a vehicle to let you know what you've done wrong, plain and simple. Anybody who tells you otherwise is not being truthful."

"People want to know they're doing a good job, that they're important, and they have something meaningful to offer. They want to know that somebody believes in them. Sometimes that's all people get out of their job. They may not have the best work environment, the best setup, or the best way to make a living. But, at the very least, they can be told that they matter. They can be told that they make a difference. And they can be encouraged to continue to do good work and be a part of something."

Lisa said, "I can't emphasize enough how important the context of encouragement is. You can't just tell somebody that they're doing a good job without having any relationship with them, or that encouragement will fall on deaf ears. They will know you don't mean it. And even if you do mean it, they won't trust that your words have any depth. Encouragement has to come in the context of a relationship that has had some time to develop, especially if you want what you're saying to resonate."

"Now," she said, taking a breath for a moment, "if you're encountering somebody for the first time, and you tried to connect with them, you assessed what their issue was, listened to their concern, and you've responded to them accordingly, your encouragement may be, 'Thank you, I really appreciated this exchange, and I look forward to talking to you again.' Something like that. And that's fine. As long as you're genuine, they'll get your sincerity. As is the case in any relationship, the level of trust will increase over time. And, as a result, so will the depth of the meaning behind your words."

I tried to take all of this in. When she spoke with such conviction, I could tell how important it was for her that I especially learn this point.

"Fred." Lisa looked right at me, pointed her finger and said, "Encouragement can help deepen a connection. When you have an opportunity to give someone praise, take it. Yes, it may at first be received with some suspicion. Over time, as the relationship develops, that will pass and your encouragement will be more deeply felt. So when you see a chance to offer a kind word, offer it. But bring it from your bones. Let your spirit drive the sentiment. That's what will begin a connection and deepen an existing relationship."

She took off her apron, put it behind the counter, looked over her shoulder at the clock, and said, "Listen, I need to get going. Try this one out with your customers and staff again, and get back to me in a week."

# CHAPTER TWELVE

Taking in everything that Lisa said, I took my time getting back to the office. When I walked through the door, our receptionist, Ellen, made eye contact with me., Just as I passed her desk, she hung up the phone and said, "Good morning, Fred. How's your day going?"

Ellen has been the receptionist at this office for at least ten years. We have had literally hundreds of conversations about difficulties with challenging customers. We've gotten to know one another pretty well. She's excellent at her job. I've never seen anyone hustle and be so good with the phones and people coming through the door as she's been all these years. And as that thought came to mind, it occurred to me that, in all of the contact I've had with her, I've never told her any of what I've just told you.

I stopped in front of her desk and said, "You know, Ellen, I just wanted to tell you that I think you are amazing at your job. I could no more do your job than I could run a marathon. I mean that sincerely. You do a magnificent job out here, and I want to make sure you know that."

Her expression said it all: Abject shock. And as I turned to go down to my office, I heard her say to her office mate, "No one has ever said that to me."

I stopped. No one had ever said that to her? Seriously? I stopped, turned and looked back at Ellen, and I could see a tear forming in her eye. She saw that I noticed it and, with a hint of embarrassment, wiped it away quickly and shuffled a few papers on her desk.

I walked back to her desk, stood in front of her, and said, "Ellen, it should have been said a long time ago. You and I have known each other a long time. You certainly see me running in and out of this office, in the morning and at night, and we talk to one another just about every day."

I felt myself shift my weight from one foot to another. I took a deep breath. I began to feel a little humbled. I could hear my voice soften and said, "I'm getting to know some new concepts about communication in these last few weeks, and one of the biggest thing I've learned is that people don't get enough appreciation or encouragement. Most of the time we barely feel like we are even noticed." I stopped for a moment and looked down at the floor. I didn't know what to say, and then thankfully these words came into my head: "I just want to make sure you know that I am really glad you're here. I hope that's okay with you."

Yeah, I know it sounds awkward. I didn't feel I was terribly prosaic in my expression. But I'm just starting this stuff out. It's seemed a little clumsy, but I really meant it and it felt like it was coming directly from my heart.

Another tear formed in Ellen's eye. She took a deep breath and said, "Fred, that's the nicest thing anybody has ever said to me in all the years that I've worked at this company." And with that, she got up out of her chair, walked around her desk, and gave me a hug.

I did not expect this. She gave me one of those really hard, squeezing hugs, with my arms pinned against my sides. All that I could do was kind of raise my forearms up from my elbows, and give her one of those pat, pat, pat hugs from my wrists.

She sat back down and wiped her eyes. I went back to my desk. I just sat there quietly, thinking that I'd done something good. I'd made somebody feel better.

Over the next few days, I noticed something was different. Every time I got on the phone or visited a customer, things seemed to go more smoothly. I didn't feel as intense. I didn't feel rushed or anxious. My stress level was down. I'll tell you something else: when I had a conversation with a customer, it went on a little longer. I wasn't so focused on the sale. I mean, let's be honest, that's why I had called, but I found I was more interested in what the person had to say. I truly enjoyed the company of the people I was on the phone with, or, sitting across the table with, having a cup of coffee.

I had never interacted with people like this before. I truly hadn't. I just followed what Lisa had said: Watch every person like you're watching a loved one. Experience them for that moment, like you're "taking in" a movie. Connect with people. Assess and listen well. Respond with meaning. Be encouraging and affirming in every conversation.

And that's what I did.

After a few days, I felt like a different person in so many ways. My sleep was better (had I known THAT would improve, I'd have done this whole thing years ago.) My conversation seemed more deliberate and more meaningful. I gave other people the chance to talk. I found myself laughing more. And the people I talked to laughed more as well.

My sales increased. The atmosphere in the office seemed to lighten.

And I felt great.

# CHAPTER THIRTEEEN

The next day as I sat down, I checked my appointment calendar and realized I hadn't set up my next appointment with Lisa. I wrote a note to call just as I opened my laptop and my phone rang. My boss called me into his office again. My first thought was, "come on, right now?" And the same stuff began to run through my head: "It's first thing in the morning. I'm trying to get back into my groove, I'm talking to customers and connecting, and I'm keeping all of Lisa's instructions in my head, and now this." Then, I took that breath that comes with "Watch" and thought about him as somebody I want to connect with, somebody that I want to "Experience" within our conversation, just taking in his energy and connecting the best I can. He's my boss, he's a person just like you and me, and—well, I was still nervous. And I was reacting to his call based on our last conversation.

I like the guy. I mean, from what I can tell, he seems OK. It's not that his call is ever welcome. It's just that the last time I had a conversation with this guy, he told me I'd be back on the street, mostly working against the draw, which made me feel like my days were numbered. So as I'm trying to apply Lisa's formula, I have this thought in the back of my head.

But this time is different. I'm better now. I'm thinking, step by step, "Watch him like you're looking at your Mom, Experience his energy and just take in what he has to say…"

I walk into his office and sat down. I'm calm…ish, but good. "Fred," he said, looking down into a manila folder with the quarterly sales report inside of it. And the fear showed up again, pushing my thoughts of kindness toward him to the back of my consciousness. His tone was dismissing, his eye contact absent, and he's got a prop to make a point. Not sure what the point is, but the quarterlies? Big deal. I've seen one million of these.

My thoughts went totally and completely out the window. I couldn't focus; I was bending to the stress, and my anxiety was increasing. I was beginning to get upset, but mostly at myself.

I'm thinking two things. Either he's going to fire me, or tell me how these sales reports are down. That something has to be done immediately, or he may be forced to make some drastic changes. All higher-ups use the same expressions. He takes a forced breath to punctuate his concern; they all do. I wonder if "how to breathe" is part of the manager's training manual. He fingers through the folder like its a prop. Come on. Is there no creativity in middle management anymore?

"Fred, these quarterly sales results are a bit troubling. I've gone over them with upper management, and we've come to the same conclusion: If we can't turn these around immediately, I'll be forced to make some drastic changes." Wow, there's a surprise. His expressionless face is the color of alabaster. If you ask me, it matches his personality.

I give him some canned response showing my concern. I try to fake sincerity and express my commitment to doing a better job. He says something unintelligible back to me, and I leave with a pasted-on look of determination and a nod, thereby showing some tacit agreement with his assessment. I assure him I'll get things going right again, or some such blather, and I leave.

As I'm walking back to my office, my blood begins to percolate. I sit down in my chair, look at my computer screen, and I put my right hand on my stapler. I pull this thing back as I lean away from my desk, and it's all I can do to keep myself from firing this sucker out the window.

Just when I needed to do the whole, "Watch, Experience, Connect…" thing, I blow it. I let my fear and anger get the better of me. This doesn't make sense. All of these steps Lisa has been sharing with me have been working. My connections with people have been improving, and my tone and approach with people are more friendly and insightful than at perhaps any other time in my career. What just happened? And are those quarterlies really accurate?

I figured there would be a jump in sales. I know I've made some good contacts in the time I've been training with Lisa, and I'm positive that my boss has seen these improvements. I've gotten along better with everybody in the sales department, and my customers really like me.

Still somewhat upset, I grab the first thing my eyes see—the folder with the notes from all the meetings I've had with Lisa. In an effort to distract myself and calm down, I go over the notes I've been taking throughout this training process at the restaurant. I'm hitting the big points, "watch, experience, connect, assess, and respond," although really I'm just trying to focus on something other than the disappointing words from my boss.

I believe in Lisa's approach; she certainly had convinced me that her stuff works, I just need to reset myself. I wanted to slowly, gradually, deliberately apply this technique to the people I came in contact with, in person and on the phone, in my office and in the hallway. I want to calm down. And as I'm taking a deep breath, centering myself, drawing forth the energy to continue this process, my boss calls me into his office, again.

Swell.

I walked into his office and sat down. And I was pretty sure what he was going to say, but he seemed a little anxious. But when he said the next words, I understood immediately why there was fear in his eyes.

"Ivan Trumble. He's coming over. Do you mind?"

Ivan Trumble is the company's largest shareholder. His pockets have floated this boat for years. He is on the board of the parent company. We're a subsidiary, and he visits all of the subsidiary companies with regularity. A difficult man. He always has a problem and never seems happy. Ivan Trumble's nickname within the sales force is, "I'm In Trouble," because whenever you hear his name uttered in any context, you generally are. In the past, when he visited the company, he threw his weight around a little. He had kind of a drill sergeant approach to communicating his concerns.

There have been more than a few occasions when Trumble has come by, spoken to one of our staff members and within a week that staff member was dismissed. This guy held a lot of power in the company. And if you didn't say what he wanted to hear, you could suffer the consequences.

So, within the past two years, we have put together a plan to respond to his issues, and it seems to work. Somewhat scripted, it always seems to calm him down. There is a lot of the "We absolutely understand your concerns, sir," and "yes, we see that these are of the utmost importance to the bottom line. and we will report to you immediately about the changes we will enact to correct these issues." It bought us a day or two to figure a decent response that would address the issues and keep him mollified. To keep it streamlined, a few of us take turns to meet him and listen to his concerns and make sure they are brought to management's attention.

Once they get it, they contact him the next day or two with a plan of action to address his concerns.

So, when the boss said, "do you mind," I knew he meant "Do you mind sitting with Trumble this time around?"

The boss takes a few minutes and explains the issue. Apparently Trumble had seen the quarter's sales dip, and he is a little more agitated than normal.

So I went back to my office and waited.*

I didn't need to wait long. Within a half hour, Trumble showed up. The boss got me on the phone, told me he was there, and said to meet him at the door. There was a conference room adjacent to the front hallway. I met Mr. Trumble at the door, shook his hand, walked him into the conference room, and sat down. The scripted responses immediately came to mind. I had planned to fall back on the old

"We'll make sure we take care of this" line and "No, problem, sir. I'll get right on that" kind of blather.

But, instead, I went for broke. I got all this instruction from Lisa, and I thought I'd just didn't have anything to lose. I wanted to be genuine. I wanted to be sincere. And I really wanted to get past all that canned verbiage we're supposed to deliver. It almost makes my mouth hurt to say it. I put all of that aside. I decided to use Lisa's formula to communicate with this man, person to person, with no pretense or formulated responses, and then hang on to see what happens.

As I'm looking into Trumble's face, I'm thinking, "Lisa, everything you've taught me better work. Because other than what you've given me, I've got nothing."

I sit down and take a quick glance around the room. I look back at Trumble and I see the kind of suit he's wearing. I study the expression on his face and try to watch everything about him. I take my deep breath, and I'm resting into the first two points, "Watch and Experience." I look at him as a beloved friend, and take in his energy. And I'm relaxed.

Trumble adjusts his suit coat and looks back across the table at me. I'm just experiencing the moment, "taking in" what he's presenting to me. I'm getting ready to hear what he has to say. In the back of my head, again I'm thinking, Watch. Experience."

I find myself smiling. I hear Lisa's voice in the back of my head, guiding me along this path.

Trumble shoots a scowl at me from underneath his eyebrows and says something about these last sales statistics being "troubling." He said that last quarter's production was discouraging, stating that he had known about the shakeup in the sales department, and the administration shift that took place not long ago.

"Now, as I understand it, you are back on the sales force. Correct?" Trumble raised his head with an expression of disdain.

I want to "connect" but I'm shifting into "assess" mode. I want to find out what he needs right now. I'm listening but I have to respond, since he just asked me a question.

"Yes sir, I am now part of the sales force. I assure you, I would give every customer's concern, and particularly your own, my utmost attention and care." Connected. Formal, almost canned, I grant you that. But I was responding to the formality in his tone and demeanor. I looked him right in the eye, and I smiled, and I felt like I was smiling genuinely. It mattered that I connect with this man. I absolutely had to assess his needs and respond to his specific issues.

Trumble said, "Good, Fred. With your history of sales behind you, I'm sure you can get us out of this mess. I wasn't too pleased that you were placed on the street, given that you hadn't been out there for a while, but I know you will do something important to change this company's trajectory." I was kind of impressed that he knew about my sales' history and that he felt I could make a difference.

But his response had emotion within it. Seemed nicer than I'd remembered him being when I met him years ago. He said, "I wasn't too pleased..." There it was. That was my opening. I could now inch more closely and more gracefully toward "connect." I stuck my head out into the conversation a little and said, "I have been doing well since I re-joined our sales force, and I even took it upon myself to get some additional training on sales technique for some continuing education. I want to help the company as much as I can."

"Oh," said Trumble, sounding somewhat curious about what I had just said, "What kind of continuing education?"

I said, "Well, Mr. Trumble, I have been taken on by a woman who is a very successful entrepreneur. She has introduced me to a six point program to some of the basic sales and customer service communication techniques. I wanted to make sure I could successfully reintegrate myself back into an active sales, service and enhanced communication environment for the optimum support and success of our company."

OK, that might have been a little much. There was a lot of "corporate speak" in there. Trumble just sat there, looking at me. So I went on.

"Sir, the program's components are as follows: "Watch, Experience, Connect, Assess, Respond and Encourage." I then explained the program in detail for a few minutes, and then talked about how I was applying it to the customers, my staff, and my colleagues. "Although it's only been in place for a short time, I have seen how my staff, colleagues and my customers have responded with a more positive outlook and relaxed response. The relationships have improved dramatically and, as a result, the communication has become clearer, easier, and more accurate. I am now able to respond to them more completely and engage in my communication with them more genuinely and with more attention to their specific needs."

Yes, I actually spoke just like this. It seemed a little stiff, but I got the point across. I told him about the whole program.

Trumble sits back in his chair, gets a little smile on his face, and says, "Well, I like it. Tell me more about this program and how you think it will help things change around here."

All I have is what I've been doing. It's the only card I have to throw. I look back at Trumble and decide to go all in.

Incorporating Lisa's formula, I say to him, "I reconnect with my customers, sir. As I mentioned, the program that I was given is broken up into six parts: Watch, Experience, Connect, Assess, Respond and Encourage. I resolve to give my customers and, for that matter, every person who crosses my path, my time and my interest as a human being, and I treat them as such. I want to get to know each one as a person, not just somebody that can offer this company a sale. I want to get to know who they are as an individual, what their interests are, and what guides that interest to our products, our service, and our staff. I want to know precisely their needs, not just so I can respond to our exchange of commerce, but as a reflective of their unique circumstances, responding to both their needs in business and their needs as a human being." I can see Trumble's face relax, so I continue.

"And when they hear my voice on the other end of the phone, I want them to hear the voice of the person that cares about them, understands their issues completely and with discernment, responding to each particular concern with the unique solution that they would expect in any relationship that is built on caring, respect, patience, attention, and kindness. I'm not just there for the sale, sir. That's not my sole objective. I'm there for the relationship. I recognize and deeply understand that the sale is the goal. That's what keeps us in business. But without the relationship, I firmly believe that sale will never be achieved and the goal of a continuing relationship has no hope of being sustained."

As I said that last sentence, Trumble raised his eyebrows and sat back in his chair. He brought his hands together over his chest, and paused for what seemed minutes, looking down at the table in front of him. Leaning back in his chair, Trumble took his eyes off the table, raised his head, and looked at me.

He took a deep breath and said, "Okay." He paused. A silent, deliberate stare focused on the table's edge. He then looked at me, offering only a glance, and said, "Okay, Fred. That's fine."

And then, another long period of silence.

He nodded, eyes fixed at the table, as if he was figuring out the last lines of a crossword puzzle.

And watching him, connecting with his expression, his posture, and the time he's been taking in just pondering these last points in our conversation, I decided in that second to reach out, to treat him not as this company's biggest investor, but as a guy sitting across the table.

I say, "Mr. Trumble, does something concern you? Is there anything I can help you with?" I wanted to say more, but I didn't want to overplay my hand. I felt I'd already done that with being so open, so I wanted to make sure I was short and direct, yet leave him open to respond as much and as long as he liked.

Trumble seemed to awaken. He went back into being the company's biggest shareholder, not the relaxed man listening while sitting at a big table. He looked at me, adjusted himself in his chair, and said "No, no, Fred, but I appreciate the question. The only trouble I have is this report and the ongoing financial support of this company. I come to visit this and other subsidiaries to see how my money is doing, and I believe it is my responsibility to find a sense of direction for the investments I've made. Meetings like this help me get a sense of that direction."

I nodded in agreement, keeping my eye contact with Trumble, and said, "Well, I will be here for you, Mr. Trumble. If there is anything I can ever do, here is my card. By all means, ring me up if there's anything I can help with."

Trumble smiled at the gesture. He got up, shook my hand, and thanked me. I thanked him back and told him I hoped to see and meet with him again, and I meant it. Being with him allowed me a little glimpse into the person, not just the shareholder.

Then he stopped at the door. "Fred," he said, "Send me an overview of that program you explained. Fax it and email it over to me before you leave today. I'm going to go over it and show it to a few people. I think we've got some potential here, and I'd like to see how it's received." I held my mouth together to keep it from falling open from shock. "Yes, sir. Happy to oblige."

Trumble gave me his fax number and his email address. I said I'd have it to him right away. I went back to my desk, took out the notes I'd collected from Lisa's training, and put them together. Ten pages, single spaced, and ran to the fax machine. Took me about an hour. I didn't realize I could type so fast.

As I went back into my office and sat back in my chair. I could feel this sense of ease come over me.

I got a text from my boss. It read, "How did it go?"

I texted back, "Everything went fine. I'm looking forward to seeing him again."

The rest of the week was full of good calls, appointments, and contacts. It was one of the best weeks I've had at the company. I was reenergized and feeling that I had really hit my stride. I am using Lisa's techniques, and I really felt I connected with Trumble.

Monday morning came, and the Boss set our meeting up for Friday. No problem, I thought, this is going to be exactly when things begin to look up. Maybe I'll get an idea of when I get back to managing a crew again. For the first time, I was really looking forward to seeing him.

Friday came, and I got the call to be in his office around noon. I showed up, maybe a couple of minutes early, and waited outside. He was on the phone, but he stepped out and waved me in. When I got into the office, he had me sit down and close the door. Just as I thought he was going to go over some kind of plan about Trumble and how to approach him in the future, he sits down behind his side of the desk.

"You know, Fred, meetings like this are never easy. Finding the right words is just so difficult…."

Suffice it to say that he didn't want to hear about the meeting about Trumble, or how I used Lisa's program, or how glistening and sharp I'd been with all my customers throughout the week. He didn't really let me speak.

Not that I could, though. My throat was closed and my mouth was dry. My head spun. I couldn't comprehend, let alone believe, what he was telling me.

I tried to slow down his words in my head so I fully understood, but I couldn't. I just closed my eyes, shook my head, and left his office. I couldn't look at his face, and I couldn't shake his hand. I just got up and left.

He fired me.

## CHAPTER FOURTEEN

I was stone cold numb.

The guy brings me in and shows me the quarterlies. I get that they were off. Did he blame me? Then, he has me meet with Trumble who has the same concerns about the sales. Got it. It has never been a big deal. We just do different things to get the sales back up. And my boss had to have heard the context of my conversation with Trumble, so why fire me? I did not know what to make of all this. Maybe the guy really didn't like me. Maybe it was his goal to kick me to the curb the minute he took over my old position and demoted me.

Either way, I was out. And absolutely stunned.

I don't exactly remembered what happened next. I know I got a box for my stuff, and I'm pretty sure I said goodbye to somebody. All I remember is sitting in my car, waiting to go someplace, and not knowing exactly where.

I decide to go to the restaurant. I pull out of the parking lot, and the numbness fades. I begin to awaken, fully realizing what just happened. I'm now wondering how this all came about and I am getting more and more upset. Was this all on my boss or Trumble? How did I get myself into this?

Maybe that whole "six point program" thing just cost me my job. I mean, who deals in this stuff? If I hadn't been listening to Lisa, I never would have spoken to Trumble that way. I have had years of experience. It's not as if I had completely forgotten how to speak to people.

I was drawing forth the kind of anger that gets people arrested. I had never felt this upset before.

As I drive over to the restaurant, I'm trying to calm myself, but my thoughts are all over the place. I pull up to the restaurant and I see Lisa through the window. I get out of my car and slam the door shut. A couple people at a nearby table raise their heads to see what the noise is all about.

The restaurant is open for another hour. A few people are finishing what is left of their meal when I see Lisa coming around the end of the counter to greet me. "Hey, this is a surprise." She tilted her head and slowed her gait as she came closer to where I was standing. Looking at me with quizzical concern, she said, "Is everything okay?"

Her kind expression and gentle tone always draw in my focus. Just seeing her took my anger down a step. Feeling a little confused, I looked away and quietly say, "I'm sorry. I think I failed." The wind just sailed out of me. As soon as I saw her, my anger left me. She could see I was deflated, or at least I think she did. "Well," she said with that understanding tone of hers, "Let's take a minute and talk about how things have gone when we close. But until then, how about you grab a pot of coffee and warm up some of the customers' cups?

So I do just that. I went behind the counter, grabbed a coffee pot, and as I come back to the tables, I stop. I look at the collection of faces sitting at the table right in front of me and I think to myself, Oh, no. You have got to be kidding me. Not today. Please, God, make this a dream.

Take a guess which customers were sitting at the table. Any wild guess will do.

If you guessed, "An assemblage of Orcs from the Lord of the Rings Trilogy?" Well, you would've been close. But, no, it was far worse.

It was the Concrete Marshmallows.

The first guy sees me and says, "Hey, darling, you're not wearing your dress today." The second guy says, "But your hair still looks just as pretty." And as I get closer to the table, the third guy says, "Hey, Sweetheart, how are ya'?

Against my better judgment, yet consistent with my mood, I walked over to the last man and calmly said, "Would you like some coffee?"

And as he said, "Sure, Honey," I craned my elbow, tilted the pot, and poured a little bit of very hot coffee directly into his cup—and a little bit into his lap. Well, maybe more than just a little bit.

Imagine a big dump truck. Now picture the big dump truck wearing a dirty blue T-shirt, gray overalls, and a cap. Just put that image in your mind. Now, take that dump truck image and visualize it jumping straight into the air with the grace of a baby gazelle. Stay with that for a minute.

Before the rest of the men at this table turned on me with the intent of removing my head from my neck, Lisa came up behind me. She calmed down the table, separated me from the rest of the group, looked at me, and said, "Go back behind the counter."

As the table calmed itself, she came back to where I was standing. Standing directly in front of me, Lisa looked me square in the eyes and calmly said, "Tell me what just happened here."

I don't know if it was what she said, the way she said it, or the culmination of the morning of events that were sounding off between my ears, but something in that moment absolutely took the wind out of my sails. I felt humiliated. I mumbled, "The coffee pot must have slipped" under my breath but as I raised my head, she knew that wasn't the case. I took a deep breath and said, "I'm sorry. I didn't mean to do that," which was a big fat lie. Then I felt myself crumble. Fighting back the feelings of frustration and emotional exhaustion, I said, "I don't know what to do anymore. I just got fired today. I'm sorry."

I could feel myself become more and more dejected. I looked over at the Marshmallows and they were readjusting themselves into their seats while one of the waitresses was attending to their needs.

"Come on into my office," Lisa said. "Tell me what happened." I sat down across from her. She sat leaning over toward me. She was concerned. Still upset with my coffee maneuver, but still wanted to know what just happened. "I have done everything you've told me to do. I have tried to watch and experience my environment, no matter where I am. I have tried to connect with people the best I could. I've assessed their needs. And I've responded as opposed to reacting, I've been really encouraging, no matter what stresses, no matter what the difficulties were in the essence of any communication."

After letting this all out on her, Lisa stopped me. She said, "OK, I think I get the picture. I have a lot to ask you and talk about, but it's late and I have a few appointments. Come over tomorrow morning. That work for you?" So kind, even in my state of temporary insanity.

Dejectedly, I said, "Well, I won't have anywhere else to go, so that'll work."

We decided on 9:30, just after the breakfast rush. I got into my car, turned the key, and headed home.

I had never felt this badly, this sad, and this much of a failure.

## CHAPTER FIFTEEN

I did not sleep much that night.

When I arrived at the restaurant in the morning, I'm sure it showed. Lisa got us both some hot water for tea, grabbed a couple of tea bags, and sat at the table by the door. "You look like you could use a little rest. Come on, sit down for a few." I want to make a note here. She took a deep breath, looked down at her teacup, and said, "Fred, when I saw you come into the restaurant yesterday, I could see that you were really angry. You caught yourself when you saw me and told me you were fired. I'm glad we had a chance to catch up yesterday. But there's a couple of things I need to talk to you about. I need to explain a little bit about your behavior."

"You're not the only one who's gotten upset or impatient at the rate of results they achieve. I know a little about where anger comes from. I've had my own issues with it over the years, given everything I had to deal with in my professional career. I faced a lot of obstacles."

"But let me share with you what I discovered, Fred. Anger primarily comes from two places: Fear and Sadness. Fear and sadness are two of our primary emotions. Anger is a response both to protect us from further fear or deepening sadness, as well as an expression that jettisons us out of those two very fundamental and raw emotions.

"Most the time anger is expressed when we don't get our way. It's pretty simple. Our expectations are not met in one form or another. We want to see things go a certain way, but they fall short of what we hoped for. We expect people to act in a certain fashion, and they don't. Fear, or sadness in one form or another, rises up. And this fear or sadness begins to take hold."

"But, she said, "Our first level of expression is frustration. We don't express our fear or sadness directly. It's difficult to do emotionally. It makes us feel too vulnerable, too exposed. Instead, we can withdraw, we can get either depressed or anxious, but more often than not we get angry. It's a protective mechanism, in a way, and it gives force to our expressions. We get angry that things don't go our way, but the source of the feeling—the fear or sadness—is always the same.

"In your case," Lisa said, taking a sip of tea, "you expected to stay behind the desk for the rest your life. Certainly, you did not expect your boss to demote you. You absolutely didn't expect him to come back and tell you that heads would roll if sales didn't improve. And you most certainly didn't expect to be fired. But you need to be clear on this point. You didn't get angry when you first came in here, at least not at first."

I disagreed. I still held that sense of shame and humiliation so closely that I felt it was best to just to keep my mouth shut, but I went against my better judgment. I corrected her.

"No," I said, "I was definitely angry."

"No," Lisa said, "you were afraid."

She was right, of course. That anxiety I first experienced when I first went in my boss's office was 100 percent undiluted fear.

"But fear comes from the ego. Fear is an ego state. It has nothing to do with our essence as a person.

"I've been trying to find a sign to put up on the wall for this one, but I haven't found one. I may make it one day, just so people have this reminder. It's about the word "ego." You know it stands for?

At this point I'm scrambling for some Freudian explanation of the meaning of the word "ego," and I'm flustered. I can't find the right words, so I said something like, "I think so."

"The word, "ego" stands for "Easing Goodness Out." Nice. I made a note of that. "But what I was a little shocked at is how easily you gave into that fear. After all, we had spoken about centering your communication from your heart—your spirit, if you will. I would've hoped that if disappointment came your way, you would draw into that spirit, and into your faith, to help you get through the tough times."

Then Lisa said something I will always remember. "Fred, although I told you the first day you walked in here that I was going to take you through a six-point spiritual journey, I don't usually talk about a person's spirituality much because I feel it's a private issue between themselves and whomever or whatever they consider their higher power. Allah, Buddha, Mohammed, Krishna, Christ, Mother Earth, Father Sky, The Field of Infinite Potentiality, it really doesn't matter to me. It's important that there be a sense of connection with something greater than themselves. But, in addition, I want people to know that there has to be a semblance of faith in who they are and how they move through this life. We have to have faith in ourselves, Fred, and when fear takes hold, faith leaves. You were afraid that day. You were afraid of those things that can happen to you given your boss's response. You were afraid the results of our meetings weren't going to occur fast enough for changes to be made at work. And I understand that."

Lisa smiled and cleared off our cups into the dish bin behind the counter. She made her way to the door. "Look at that sign above the door." I looked up and saw it say, "When Fear Knocks at the Door, and Faith Answers, Nobody's There."  Lisa said, "Whatever gives you a sense of faith in yourself, and even in a Higher Power, I'd access a little of that throughout this week."

"Which brings me to my next question." she said, "What do you plan on doing with yourself for the next few weeks?"

I had no ready answer, so I said, "I'm going to look for a job, I guess."

She said, "Well, that's not a bad idea." Then she asked me something that was completely unexpected. "Do you want to continue the training?" Without thinking, I reflexively said, "Sure! Can I come here every week?"

"How about every day?" Lisa said, "Here's what I have in mind. When people have lost their jobs—and it's happened a few times—I've had them come to the restaurant, work through their job searches on their computers, and get to know the people here. You want to stay engaged. By just speaking with people and getting to know who they are, you're becoming a better, more caring person. Most importantly, you're focusing on them and not on yourself. In that spirit, you can practice the six points I've spoken to you about while you're having coffee and getting to know the customers.

Lisa fumbled for her ignition key, looked me straight in the eyes and said, "But I need a favor.

When you get here for your first day, your first order of business is apologizing to the Marshmallows."

I smiled. "You're right. No problem. Thanks." As she got into her car, she rolled down her window and said, "And, one last thing: Remember that sign above the door, Fred. Make that your mantra from here on out. It'll take you out of your ego. And your anger will disappear." Then she drove away.

And I could hear myself repeat within my head the words of the sign above the door: "When Fear Knocks at the Door, and Faith Answers, Nobody's There."

## CHAPTER SIXTEEN

The first day in, feeling very humbled and contrite, I apologized to the Concrete Marshmallows. I stuck out my hand to shake theirs, and they were surprisingly gracious. Every one of them reached out and shook my hand in return.

Each day throughout the following weeks I got to know some of the regulars. Nice people with interesting lives. I'm a sucker for a good story, so the days passed easily. I practiced the strategies that Lisa has taught me every conversation I'd had. I'd begun to make it a habit.

Slowly, Lisa became conversant, even commenting on some of the exchanges I had with her customers. She made some small talk with me and brought out some strategies within the training. We didn't spend any time together, per se, but we did speak nearly every day. And, truth be told, that kept me coming back. The conversations with Lisa helped keep me focused, and the practice within the restaurant helped me make new friends. I'd really looked forward to coming to the restaurant. I was adopting and perfecting an entirely new way to communicate.

As I was beginning my sixth week of the job search, a customer came in and sat down at the counter. He was in a nice suit and cut a very professional figure. He looked like somebody that worked in my office. When Lisa came over and asked him what he would like, he said, "Oh, just coffee for now."

As he was handed his cup, he jostled his coffee for just a second, and a big splash of brown liquid landed squarely in the middle of his tie. "Oh, damn," he said, "I've got a meeting this morning." Looking to me, he said, "Do you know of any one-hour dry cleaners around here?"

I didn't, but from my years spent on the road visiting clients, eating in a hundred different places, I always carried a couple of pressed ties in a box in the trunk of my car just in case of emergencies like this.

"No, I don't know of any cleaners," I said, "but I've got a couple of ties in my car. They're both pressed, and one goes well with your suit. Give me a second."

I headed out to my car, grabbed both ties, and came back into the restaurant. He was turned around on his stool as I'm coming through the door.

"Here you go," I said, "take your pick."

He saw the one I was thinking about and reached for it. "This is amazing," he said. "Thank you so much," and went back into the restroom to change.

When he came out, he shook my hand, and said, "You know, I better get going. I think I might just make it to that meeting early. Are you going to be here tomorrow? I wanted to make sure I get you back your tie."

"Keep it. It's a gift. But, yes, I'll be here tomorrow," I said, reaching out my hand for his. "I'm Fred."

"I'm Juan. I'll be here around the same time tomorrow, if that's OK with you." We argued over his accepting the gift of the tie for a bit before my insistence won over. He said, "Then at least let me buy you breakfast tomorrow." I agreed.

Juan appeared at 10:00 the next morning. I thanked him for buying my breakfast. He thanked me for the tie. After I "watched" and "experienced" how he came over to me, smiled, and shook my hand, I went straight for the connection.

I mentioned how impressed I was with his hand/eye coordination in handling coffee cups. That made him laugh. I liked the guy. And the connection had begun. He told me he worked for a firm in their management team a the corporate headquarters, but he made his career in sales. General answer, and that was fine. I told him that I'd spent a lot of years in sales, too, and we started swapping stories of the road.

But the talk slowed a little. When I asked him if he liked his job, he paused and said, "Yeah, I guess. I've been there only a couple of months, so I'm adjusting." He was tentative in the way he formed his words. I could tell that he was suddenly preoccupied, and even worried about something. I was wondering where the source of the pressure came from, so I asked him.

Lisa had already taken our orders and came around to refill our coffee cups. She quickly looked at me, smiled at him, and then hurried to wait on other customers.

Juan said, "Budget changes, management issues, sales are off, that kind of thing. Overseeing a good deal of our clients now, so it's just something to get used to."

I told him I knew exactly what he meant. With his tense expression beginning to relax a little, I asked him what issues were the most troubling.

"Well," he said, "I'm trying to reestablish some connection, offer some added depth in the relationships with my clients. I want to put a new energy into my interactions with these people. Sales need to get back up, and I frankly need to be a little more involved with the sales and customer service process."

It was as if the Angel of Interpersonal Relationships sat down on the stool next to us and said, "Here, Fred. Let me toss one your way."

Lisa walked past us and tended to something behind the counter. Her back was to both of us. But as Juan finished his sentence, Lisa looked directly at me, grinned—I'm thinking she must have overheard what he just said—and went to wait on a couple of other customers.

So, I took a quick sip from my coffee cup and said, "Juan, I need to mention something. I was pretty much in the same boat as you are not all that long ago. Thanks to a mentor, I learned this new system. It helped me connect better with my staff and my customers, and I'd be happy to teach it to you. The specifics don't take long to learn. I could even teach you over a few cups of coffee, but you'd have to practice this with your people. Then just come back to me and let me know how it went." I still had copies of the program I sent to Trumble, and I gave a set to him.

Juan looked at the copies and you could tell he was all in. "Yeah, that would be great. You have a little time today?" So, he and I went from the counter to a booth, and I started talking to him about "Watch" and "Experience."

Is this cool, or what?

## CHAPTER SEVENTEEN

Juan came in a few more times over the next couple of weeks. We had great conversations. He took to this program quickly. He said that already people were responding to him differently. Conversations were more involved, and a sense of interest was dictating every encounter. Whether on the phone or in person, Juan's ability to "connect," as he put it, was steadily growing. He seemed to take to it immediately.

"This approach is opening the doors of conversation that, frankly, were previously closed. I have learned so much about the people in my office, in the field, and particularly on my list of accounts that I am truly looking forward to going to work. It's all new, and it's early, I know, but I'm thinking about this process every day. I'm even using it with my kids!" Laughing, Juan said, "They're looking at me like, 'Who is this guy?' I mean, I've never really taken the time to speak to them as you've shown me, Fred. This has been such an eye opener." Juan had to run, but he said he'd be back in about a week. He needed to go on a business trip, but said he looked forward to getting back to the restaurant to talk.

When he came back, he was eager to get together. He called me and we set an appointment. But just before he hung up, Juan said, "When I come in with what I have to tell you, I'd recommend you be sitting down." We set up a coffee date for the next morning.

Juan came in, shook my hand, and couldn't wait to talk. "Fred," he said, "My trip was great. People were commenting on how engaged I seemed. They talked about how friendly, how interested I was in them."

"But here's the good part: When I got back into my office, I ran into my boss. I spoke to him about this program that you had been showing me, and he made an unusual comment."

"OK." I said. "Unusual, how?"

Juan said, "Well, maybe I should back up a little. A little while ago, my boss had been speaking to one of the shareholders. They had a quarterly meeting. This particular shareholder is probably the biggest one we have. He sits on the board of the parent company, has stock in a lot of subsidiaries in this area. Kind of like a Warren Buffett guy, but not as warm and far more of a micro-manager. He likes to visit the companies he's invested in about once a quarter."

Anyway, the shareholder told my boss that he spoke to a salesman at another one of the subsidiaries. He said he really liked this guy and his ability to connect. The guy even faxed the shareholder a ten-page report about the nature of the program. The shareholder said he'd fax the program to my own boss, and my boss got a copy of the program a couple of days ago."

He sipped his water and said, "Anyway, last week on his quarterly visit, the shareholder went back to the company to talk to this salesman again and find out more about his program. He was there to make the salesman an offer to head a training effort to get this program implemented company-wide. The shareholder has even talked to the Board about getting this salesman a full time position as "Head of Communications" under Corporate Sales.

"But when the shareholder contacted the man's company, he discovered they let him go." Juan broke out in a knowing smile. "The boss told me that at the end of the week, they plan to make every effort to contact this man to make him that offer."

I felt my face flush. I couldn't speak. Literally, I could not form words. I'm thinking, "No way. This isn't happening. I'm dreaming. Pinch me. Smack me upside the head. Wake me up."

I sat there motionless. Absolutely frozen. I couldn't believe what I was hearing.

"Oh, and one more thing you should know, Fred." Juan took another sip of his water and said, "The shareholder's name is Ivan Trumble. Sound familiar?"

Juan let out a laugh. He put his hand on my shoulder.

I just about fell off my stool. Literally. I lost feeling in my limbs. I was in shock. Or I just had a stroke. In that case, I was hoping old Juan here knew how to dial "911."

Juan said, "This is great. I guess that'll keep everybody from looking for you later this week!"

Juan and I shook hands and hugged each other. He said he'd call me later this afternoon to get things started.

I raised my arms over my head. I felt my face. Nope, no stroke. Whew…

I sat there for about ten minutes, staring at the counter. I just wanted to soak in what just took place. Then I looked around for Lisa.

I told her the whole story.

She said, "Sit down for a second." We sat in a booth adjacent to the counter. "You know, over those meetings with Juan, I overheard how you were teaching him the program. I was really impressed with you. You never asked him for a job, assistance, or help. You never gave him your resume and, as far as I can tell, you were entirely focused on him and his welfare. Your ego was nowhere to be found in here."

"I had hoped something like this would happen, something that would show me that you were serious, that your ego had been displaced by your feelings and concern for others."

Lisa nodded her head and said, "You really turned yourself around." And, the next thing she said just put me back on my heels. "You know, Fred, you don't need any more training. We have one more thing to go through, but it's a formality. We'll set up a time when you can get back here.

You have this thing wired. And, from what I have just seen, you've done just about as well as anyone that's been put through the program."

"So we need to tie this up. You're about to start a new job!" She said there was no hurry with the very last part of the training, "but it is an important reminder of everything you've done up to this point, and beyond. Get your feet wet in the new job and then come back and tell me how it's going. I want to know how you're doing."

I was ready to take the next step in my life and career.

## CHAPTER EIGHTEEN

The job has been fantastic. I feel like myself again. I'm really getting to know my staff. I see who they are as people and what motivates them to do quality work. Most importantly, people are demonstrating genuine care, compassion and interest in each person that crosses their path. My staff is happy, their customers are happy, profits are up, and the folks at corporate are really happy.

I haven't seen Lisa in about four weeks. I called her to catch up and thank her, and I told her about how things were going. Just as we were about to hang up, she stopped short and said, "Hey, I hope you didn't forget, but you didn't exactly finish the training." She said there was one critical piece that she needed to communicate. She asked that I come over around closing time and get, what she said, is a "symbol of what this all means."

Lisa has been extraordinary. She gave me my life back. She gave me a place to come when I had no job and nowhere else to go. She helped me reclaim myself again—only now I was a much better, more centered and empathetic person than I had been before. I was so grateful to her.

I arrived at the restaurant as she was closing. She was already looking at me, smiling. "Today, my friend, your training is officially completed."

She said my face was more relaxed, that my expression was more confident. I was really pleased to hear this, and I was beginning to trust her judgment. I know it sounds like it took me a while, but I was still learning a great deal through this new chapter of my life.

"Well," Lisa said, "You have learned and incorporated a new technique that finally comes from your heart. And now all you need to do is to tie it all together."

I wasn't sure what she meant. I thought I had it all together, but as I reached for my next syllable, Lisa said, "Fred, with the foundation of The Golden Rule, you learned this: W-E-C-A-R-E: Watch, Experience, Connect, Assess, Respond, Encourage. WE—you, me, and every person in this restaurant, every colleague you encounter, and every customer you reach—set the format of life's interactions and experiences. Life is about all of us, together. It is inclusive. This is the collective "WE." All of life's journeys grow from all of us, together."

"You establish relationships with your staff and your customers because you "CARE." You treat others with compassion, straight from the heart. People matter, now more than they ever have."

I stood there a little dumbfounded. My first thought was that I was really impressed with how she knitted these concepts together like this into something so clear, so easy to explain.

Then my second thought was, "An Acronym? Really? I can't stand acronyms! No wonder I missed it. Acronyms are just so overused, so annoying.

But I had to admit, this one was brilliant. And it hit all the points effortlessly.

She pulled a box from underneath the counter. I had no idea what it was. "Open it," she said. I lifted the lid, and inside was a gold bracelet. The bracelet was engraved with the letters, W.E.C.A.R.E. I put it on my wrist. "It fits." I couldn't think of anything else to say. I was humbled by her thoughtful and generous gift.

"It's a reminder. If you ever get stuck, just look down at your wrist. If you really get stuck, just give me a call. You know where to find me."

It meant so much coming from someone who had helped so many people. She had been so good to me. And now this bracelet. She took my picture and said she'd put it in the book with all her other "success stories."

"One last thing." Lisa said." W.E.C.A.R.E. is the Mission Statement. Speak it with the passion is deserves. It is a battle cry. It is the foundation that supports every word you speak now, to family and friends, to customers and colleagues. It is a declaration. Punctuate it. Emphasize it. Articulate every syllable. Make it your Clarion Call. It will guide you into all communication. It will, as you've seen, change your life."

Lisa pointed to my wrist. "It will give you everything you need."

The next few weeks were measurably happier, more engaging, and distinctly more successful than I had ever experienced. I was introduced to a variety of accounts and met the sales and customer service teams. I trained my managers in the W.E.C.A.R.E. system, sending out weekly emails on the attitudes and techniques that support each application. The firm had a monthly staff meeting when I was first there, and I was asked to introduce myself and explain my "philosophy" to the one hundred or so folks that gathered. This was not going to be like the meetings in the last firm. No phoning in the message, giving same worn out talk. Standing behind the podium, I looked out the those in attendance and said, "I'll be brief."

"One of my favorite authors and lecturers was Leo Buscaglia. I have a quote of his in a frame above the door to my office. It reads, "Too often, we underestimate the power of a touch, a smile, a kind word, an honest compliment, or the smallest act of caring, all of which have the potential to turn a life around." "It is within this spirit that I come to you today, to offer this sense of attention to one another in everything we do. It is a focused application that brings us all-our peers, our customers and, more importantly, our immediate friends and families-closer together, raising the bar for a respectful, considerate and engaged relationship with everyone in our lives, based on the compassion that is the foundation of "The Golden Rule." I explained the six steps in short detail, letting them know what each letter stood for and what it meant in application. I told them I would have a weekly newsletter in their e-mail to address these points, and that I would be conducting training as needed. Then I explained that, "The acronym of these six concept's is "W-E-C-A-R-E." I hope it contributes to a cultural shift among us all. It will show everyone-from the custodian to the chairman of the board-that they matter. The smile on our face when they catch our eye is genuine, drawn from the kinship we have with each other, bringing us together in every walk of our life. I challenge all of us to apply these changes now, beginning with the first words and expressions we offer to one another as we first meet. We will always see one another as good, allowing each other to share their thoughts and ideas with us, connecting with their presence and assessing their concepts with an open and inquisitive mind. We respond with thoughtfulness, friendship and ease, and we encourage each other to continue to be open in their exchange us. It brings forth more comprehensive and detailed sharing of information. It makes our decisions precise. And, most importantly, it deepens our trust with one another."

"Today, we attend to one another with kindness, compassion and friendship. Today, we begin anew."

"WECARE is easy. It lifts us up, it improves all aspects of our communications and encounters. It is, finally, the difference we have been waiting for. People in this company will want to stay with this company because we treat one another with more consideration and respect, so there will be little turnover. Clarity and consideration of one another will be the centerpiece of communication so decisions will be comprehensive and precise, with the depth and detail needed to go forward. Relationships will be made with one another and our customers. Our sales and productivity will greatly improve. The bottom line will rise. The morale will soar."

And the way will treat one another, in business and in very part of our lives, will change forever."

"Because WE CARE."

"Thank you."

I stepped down off the stage to a standing ovation. I don't think I'd ever gotten one of those at the old company. I probably would have remembered.

Thank you, Lisa.

Thank you so much.

| | |
|---|---|
| **"WATCH:"** | To look at someone with without judgement. |
| **"EXPERIENCE:"** | To be with them, to "take in" their presence. |
| **"CONNECT:"** | To reach toward them. To engage. |
| **"ASSESS:"** | To listen and evaluate their message. |
| **"RESPOND:"** | To offer insight a considerate and attentive fashion. |

**"ENCOURAGE:"** To let that person know that they are appreciated and valued.

www.ingramcontent.com/pod-product-compliance
Lightning Source LLC
Chambersburg PA
CBHW030942240526
45463CB00016B/1367